Under
the Influence

Under the Influence

Congress, Lobbies, and the American Pork-Barrel System

William Ashworth

Foreword by Congressman Jim Weaver

Hawthorn/Dutton ‖ New York

For information contact:
Elsevier-Dutton Publishing Co., Inc., 2 Park Avenue, New York, N.Y. 10016

Library of Congress Cataloging in Publication Data
Ashworth, William. Under the influence;
congress, lobbies, and the American pork-barrel system.
1. Corruption (in politics)—United States.
2. Patronage, Political—United States. 3. United States.
Congress. I. Title.
JK2249.A73 · 320.973 80-16373
ISBN: 0-8015-5929-4

Published simultaneously in Canada by
Clarke, Irwin & Company Limited, Toronto and Vancouver

Designed by Kingsley Parker

10 9 8 7 6 5 4 3 2 1

First Edition

Waste not, want not.
—OLD SAYING.

Waste not, want . . . oh, what the hell.
—GOVERNMENT VERSION.

Contents

Foreword

When I was a boy, my mother would often assure me that if I was good there would be a nice apple pie for dessert. Speaker Sam Rayburn used to counsel new members of the House in much the same way: "to get along, go along." The reward for such behavior was a dip into the pork barrel of public works, a dam or a bridge or a federal building for a member's district. Indeed, the pork barrel is as American as apple pie.

But the times are changing. Not many years ago, a member of Congress was universally lauded by his constituency for bringing home a federal project. Today, however, in my district and others, a dam or other piece of pork is as adamantly opposed by some as it is desired by others. To stretch the culinary metaphor further, a congressman still brings home the bacon, but now it is often seen to be adulterated with nitrosamines.

In a sense, this is too bad, because there is good in the pork barrel, too. Representative democracy is a tenuous thing. Its function is to resolve the deep and powerful conflicts which occur in any society, and which can at any time

cause the workings of our government to fly apart if cohe-
sion is lost. Gathering around the pork barrel helps make
possible the compromising that keeps the body politic
functioning. Its use is admirably illustrated by the career of
Senator Wayne Morse, one of my heroes in politics, whose
success in obtaining dams for Oregon helped him ride over
the difficulties his other more controversial policies caused
him.

The evil is not the pork barrel. The evil is that pork so
often becomes an end unto itself, with the real benefits to
society lost to individual greed.

During my first year in Congress, a powerful member of
the Public Works Committee from Texas sat down next to
me on the House floor. "Now look here," he said, knowing
mine was a strong public works district. "You want some
more dams, you vote for oil." As my politics are decidedly
against the oil companies, that might have been a real
threat. It caused me only amusement, however, as the dam
sites still left were not, in my opinion, worth the money,
and further, had serious environmental drawbacks. In fact,
I was trying to block their development.

So I did not vote for oil. The committee threatened to cut
out several public works projects under consideration for
southwest Oregon. When they discovered that that was fine
with me, a strange thing happened: they included them
anyway. The threat was a bluff. The reality was that *they*
wanted to build them. *They* are the old New Deal public-
works bulls in Congress, allied with the Corps of Engineers
whose lifeblood is building more dams. The Corps could
not exist without them.

But the pork barrel is not just dams and other public
works. The pork barrel affects virtually every decision that
Congress makes. Defense spending, for example, is now a
far larger slice of the hog than public works, and when the
Defense Appropriations bill is brought to the floor, the
bitter fights that occur are not over strategy or policy, but

between members who represent airplane manufacturers in California and those who represent airplane manufacturers in New York or Missouri. This evil not only costs Americans dearly in their pocketbooks, but in national security.

So the pork barrel has become not only wasteful, but dangerous. And that is why it must be brought under control. Not just because it has made us the most spendthrift nation on earth, but because it is making our decisions for us. And that, as Bill Ashworth so aptly demonstrates in this book, is not the way to make judgments for the good of our society.

CONGRESSMAN JIM WEAVER

Acknowledgments

My greatest debt for assistance in the creation of this book is owed to my wife, Melody, and my daughters, Jenny and Sara, for putting up with me during the sometimes difficult process of creation. It's not easy to be an author's family, but these three have usually made it look that way. I owe them enormously for being patient, supportive, appreciative, critical—and most of all, for just being.

Others whose names do not appear in the text but who contributed in a variety of important ways include my close friend, fellow writer and travel agent Bryan Frink, who superbly handled the itinerary and lodgings for my research trips; my sister Lillian, who kept an eye out for outstanding news items relating to the pork-barrel system; Greg Skillman of Congressman Weaver's staff, who served as my principal anchor in the sea of confusion that is Washington during appropriations season; and my old friend George Pollock, whose insight into things governmental is remarkable, and who very kindly provided lodging for me during the Portland (Oregon) phase of my research. I would also like to acknowledge the help, counsel, and support of at least the following: Larry Williams of the Council on Environmental Quality; Tom Schmoe, Chuck James, and John Affolter of Live Without Trident; Bill Bonvillian of the Transportation Department; Jean Allen, Richard Q. Vawter, and Walter V. Kallaur of the General Services Administration; Jim Farrell and Jim Sundquist of the Brookings Institution; Evelyn Bradshaw and Ed Snyder of the Friends Committee on National Legislation; Anne Clark of the League of Conservation Voters; Coral Beuchler of the Federal Information Center in Portland, Oregon; Willie Bradford of the Congressional Budget Office; Daisy P. Burley of the Treasury Department; William F. Sherman of the National Archives and Records Service; Walter Haase of the Office of Management and the Budget; Mark DuBois of Friends of the River; Edward C. Fritz of the Texas Committee on Natural Resources; and Peg and Albert Ormsby, Clara Mae Spray, Tom Berlin, and Ron and Matilda Fowler of the Upper West Fork Watershed Association of Lewis County, West Virginia.

Under
the Influence

1

The Pork-Barrel Polka: Hamming It Up in Washington

Lord, the money we do spend on government, and it's not one bit better than the government we got for one-third the money twenty years ago.

—WILL ROGERS

The fruits of the American government cornucopia often seem to be distributed on a highly uneven geographic basis. Certain states appear to get a far greater share of the budgetary pie than others; within individual states, certain regions and certain special interests seem blessed with especially straight and slippery pipelines into the federal treasury. It would be nice to be able to report that this appearance is illusory, but unfortunately it is not. These imbalances are real. All too often, the spending patterns of the major government agencies are set not by where the money is needed but by the structure of power in Congress: the lines of influence that determine which congressman or senator has the most clout with his colleagues in relation to the program of the agency doing the spending, and can get the biggest piece of that program for his district or

state. And the misallocation of resources—resulting in cul-
tural, social, and environmental havoc—and the sheer, unadulterated waste caused by this antiquated system are
enormous, amounting to tens of millions of dollars every
day.

Spring is spending season in Washington. Each year,
with the regularity of salmon running upstream to spawn,
the lobbyists for multitudes of local interests converge on
the nation's capital, each one eager to bend the ear of his
elected representative in favor of some pet project—a dam,
a military contract, a canal, a new federal building, an airport grant—which will funnel government money into the
representative's district or state. Usually the representative
is glad to listen, believing—validly or not—that the federal
funds spent on these projects will translate directly into
votes in the next election. If he is a member of a key committee, he ordinarily will have no trouble convincing his
colleagues to provide funds for his district. If he is one of
the low men in the congressional pecking order, he will
have a little more trouble, but he still should be able to snag
enough government bucks to impress his constituents if he
talks it up right. Some of the projects thus funded will be
needed; some will be needed, but not in that particular
location; and some will not be needed at all. But questions
of need, though regularly given lip service in committee
testimony and in floor debate, rarely enter very deeply into
the congressional decision-making process. There the key
question asked of budget items is all too often not *what is
it?* but *who wants it?*

During the dark days of American morality prior to the
Civil War, slaves on the most repressive of the southern
plantations were often kept on near-starvation rations.
However, once in a while, on a celebration day like Christmas or the Fourth of July, the plantation owner would roll
out a barrel of salt pork and invite his slaves to help themselves. This usually led to a free-for-all, as the protein-

starved slaves fought over the choicest bits of pork from the barrel. Later political observers, noting the similarities between the behavior of slaves fighting over pieces of salt pork and the deportment of congressmen and senators fighting over choice government projects, began calling appropriations bills containing such projects "pork barrels." By 1879, the term *pork* was in use on the floor of Congress; by 1890, *The New York Times* could use it in a headline without fear of being misunderstood. Most such references were derogatory, but this didn't stop the barrel, which just kept rolling along—and growing as it went. It is still with us. In 1980, according to one reliable estimate, it will cost United States taxpayers someplace in the neighborhood of $115 million every day.

At something over a half-trillion dollars annually, the federal budget of the United States government is almost literally incomprehensible in size, scope, and complexity. Even the available analogies boggle the mind. One day's worth of the current budget, converted into quarters, would make a stack nearly 6,000 miles high; one minute's worth, deposited on your doorstep as a pile of dollar bills, would make such a huge mound of money that it would take you two weeks of nonstop work just to count the stuff. Three weeks' worth would be enough to pay every single bill incurred by the federal government from the birth of the republic right up to the outbreak of hostilities in World War I. Given spending on that order of magnitude, and given the clumsy, compromise-between-committees manner in which the budget is put together, it is inevitable that a certain amount of waste creep in. What is particularly galling about the type of waste created by pork barreling, however, is not that it is inevitable but that it is not. Most pork-barrel spending is entered into with the clear knowledge that waste is going to be involved. Consider these examples:

- In Oregon, the Weather Bureau recently volunteered to save taxpayers $31,000 per year by closing the Mt. Sexton Weather Station, which it called a "nonessential site." The Subcommittee on Commerce of the House Appropriations Committee concurred, striking funds for the Mt. Sexton station from the 1980 budget. The full Appropriations Committee put them back.
- In Florida, the Army Corps of Engineers has been trying for several years to get Congress to stop asking them to complete the Cross-Florida Barge Canal. Though 70 percent of the construction work on the canal has already been done, recent Corps studies have shown that the $130 million it will take them to finish the job is considerably more than the project will produce in benefits. The army has submitted legislation to Congress every year since 1977 which would "deauthorize" the canal. Every year since 1977, the legislation has failed to pass.
- In Colorado, the Bureau of Reclamation is hard at work on a $100-million dam that critics claim will benefit exactly eighty-eight people. It has been suggested, only half-facetiously, that instead of building the dam the Bureau should take a brown paper bag with a million dollars in it to each of the beneficiaries and offer it to them tax-free—thus saving the treasury twelve million dollars. But funds for this project continue to be included in the Bureau's construction account each year with scarcely a ripple of congressional protest.

In each of these examples—and in the seemingly infinite number of others, large and small, which could be added to the list from all parts of the country—there is one common, consistent factor: the behavior of Congress. In all these cases, and in every case involving pork barreling, Congress has based its decision on how to spend the taxpayers' money not on any perception of what will be good for the nation as a whole but on what one particular congressman or small group of congressmen feels will do the most good for his constituents.

The implications of this are ominous, going far beyond the mere fact that excessive amounts of waste are involved. The truth of the matter is that the congressional budgetary process is totally out of control. With few exceptions, each congressman and senator sees as his prime fiscal responsibility not the protection of the federal treasury but the raiding of that treasury for the benefit of his state or district. And the success of his raid will have very little to do with whether or not his colleagues perceive it as a raid. Instead it will depend on the raiding congressman's position in the power structure, on how many deals he can work with other congressmen, and on the knowledge on the part of many of his colleagues that if they don't vote for his raid he won't vote for theirs. And, of course, there's the overriding fear, on the part of all 535 august and dignified members of the greatest legislative body on earth, that if they don't scramble for the bacon somebody else will. "Government spending," one critic has written, "is like a jammed faucet. The ordinary citizen can't put the water back in the faucet, so he hurries up with his tin cup."

What about reform? There are those who are trying, but most of them are not optimistic about their chances. One major hurdle is that most congressmen don't see the pork-barrel system as a problem, but as an opportunity—or even a solemn obligation. "One major facet of a congressman's duties," wrote veteran Texas Congressman Jim Wright in 1963, "is that of producing desirable results for his own district." "United Aircraft is in our district," explained an aide to Representative Emilio Daddario of Connecticut to columnists Drew Pearson and Jack Anderson in 1968. "It employs 60,000 people. It's our job to help them get business and to help the economy of the district."

The overwhelming majority of congressmen, it appears, would still agree with these assessments, a situation which does not give heart to those few members of the House and

Senate who are fighting to trim pork fat from the budget. "I see absolutely no hope for it," Congressman Jim Weaver of Oregon told me in the spring of 1979. "You see, each constituency wants their stuff, whatever it happens to be. And so there's no stopping the pork barrel, because you get back here, and you know that if you vote against somebody else's pork barrel, you lose yours, and so everybody just chips in. And the upshot is that these projects have absolutely no real checks on them." Weaver would undoubtedly agree with Senator William Proxmire of Wisconsin, the Senate's leading proponent of fiscal responsibility, who once remarked after an unsuccessful floor campaign against a pork-barrel water-projects bill that it was "like trying to make Niagara Falls run uphill—and I wouldn't be surprised to see them put *that* in a public-works bill someday."

Still, Weaver, Proxmire, and a few others keep trying. And maybe someday they will succeed. Maybe one of the reform amendments to the Constitution currently kicking around Washington—the balanced-budget amendment, the line-item-veto amendment, the voter-initiative amendment—will gather a large enough head of steam behind it to go through. Maybe Common Cause will manage to corral enough votes to pass its long-sought public-financing law for political campaigns, freeing congressmen from dependence on the contributions of the special interests who are the principal beneficiaries of pork bills. Maybe hell will freeze over. Or maybe. . . .

In the summer of 1964, the members of the Idaho congressional delegation went before their colleagues to seek passage of authorizing legislation for a massive pork-barrel project, a huge Bureau of Reclamation dam to be flung across a river near the small town of Rexburg in the southern part of the state. All the old tired clichés of pork were trotted out on the floor and dutifully reprinted in the *Congressional Record.* Senator Frank Church called it "this most important Idaho project"; Senator Len Jordan asked for the bill on the grounds that it was "important to the local economy"; Representative Ralph Harding remarked that it "enjoys unanimous support in Idaho. There has not been a single voice in Idaho raised in opposition to this much-needed project." The expected price tag was $52 million. In 1969, when construction began, it was still $52 million. Two years later, estimated costs had ballooned upward nearly 40 percent to $71 million, unofficial estimates of returns had dropped as low as forty cents on the dollar, questions had been raised about the safety of the dam site, environmentalists were suing over the loss of the local trout fishery, and the Bureau of Reclamation, admitting to grave doubts about the economic justification of the project, began to make noises about wanting out.

Congress, as usual, wouldn't let them. The dam was completed in the spring of 1976 at a cost of approximately $102 million, an overrun of nearly 100 percent. And a few weeks later, on June 5, 1976, as the reservoir was being filled for the first time, the whole thing collapsed, sending a wall of water downstream that nearly wiped out Rexburg, killing eleven people and doing an estimated $400 million worth of damage.

Maybe if we just have a few more Teton Dams . . .

The average constituent is probably not aware just how hard his representative or senator is working down there in Washington to defend him and to promote his interests over and above the interests of the rest of the republic. A congressman's day hardly ever goes by without the need for getting up in front of some committee, or on the floor of the House or the Senate, or on the phone to some high-level bureaucrat, and going to bat for some district-specific item. The item may be funds for a new flood-control project in Iowa:

> MR. GRASSLEY *of Iowa:* "I want to thank . . . the whole sub-
> committee for responding to the request of the leadership
> of the little city of Evansdale in my district for their request
> for an additional $200,000 for additional planning for the
> flood-control project there. . . . "

It may be a Department of Commerce field office in New
York which has proved uneconomic and which the department wants to close:

> MR. ROONEY *of New York:* "Do you mean that employees of
> long standing, who, for instance, live right in my congres-
> sional district . . . have no right to . . . raise their voices to
> prevent loss of jobs . . . ?"

It may be the weather report from Savannah, Georgia,
which the Weather Bureau has been distributing to New
York and Philadelphia and other northeastern population
centers as a favor to the Savannah tourist industry—a practice which the agency feels it can no longer economically
justify:

> MR. PRESTON *of Georgia:* "I wrote you gentlemen . . . a polite
> letter about it, thinking that maybe you would [restore it]
> . . . and no action was taken on it. Now, Savannah may be
> unimportant to the Weather Bureau but it is important to
> me. . . . "

That actions such as these are the rule, and not the exception, in Congress is perhaps best shown by the plaintive
remark of one Civil Aeronautics Board official at a Senate
subcommittee hearing in the early 1960s. "I cannot think,"
said the official, "of any local service case in which we have
not had at least fifteen, twenty, or twenty-five members of
Congress each one urging an extension of the local service
to the communities in his constituency as being needed in
the public interest."

Are these projects in the public interest? The answer varies from case to case. The Iowa flood-control project and some of the CAB local service requests possibly were; the extra Weather Bureau reports, the uneconomic Department of Commerce field office, and the bulk of the CAB requests almost certainly were not. But in a larger sense, the question is probably irrelevant. For the truth is that "in the public interest" is one of those wishy-washy phrases which can be defined in many ways—and of those ways, the only one of any real interest to the average congressman seems to be the one which equates "public interest" with direct benefits to his constituents.

Caught on the horn of that definition, and pushed by the nagging fear that if he doesn't produce tangible results for his state or district before the next election the voters may decide to send him into early retirement, almost every member of Congress sticks his hand into the pork barrel at one time or another. Senator Frank Church, that implacably liberal foe of the filibuster, once threatened to "hold the Senate floor as long as God gives me the strength to stand" in a filibuster of his own to prevent an Idaho pork barrel from being stricken from a public works appropriations bill. Representative Jim Weaver, whose profound and emphatic distaste for pork has already been mentioned, is the man most responsible for keeping the Weather Bureau's "nonessential" Mt. Sexton Weather Station pulling the taxpayers' dollars into his southern Oregon district. "Congressmen that you normally see as antispending will vote essentially for every agricultural subsidy that affects their state," complains David Keating of the National Taxpayers' Union, one of the most effective spending-watchdog lobbies in Washington. "The sugar beet people in Idaho, the dairy people in Wisconsin—in those two states you'll see some really antispending congressmen who will *not* vote for the end of those subsidies, and those are obviously pork barrels for their constituents."

One Texas representative summed the whole problem up concisely on the floor of the House a number of years ago. "I am for economy in Idaho and perhaps in Maine and a considerable amount down in Oklahoma," he told his colleagues. "Then in the districts of some of my [Texas] colleagues, I am for economy over there unless it would injure and hurt my colleagues; but when you come into my district I am for economy but." And, as Richard Fenno has cynically remarked, whenever that phrase crops up Congress is expected to resolve it "by tilting the balance of decision toward the 'but' and not the 'economy.'"

As nearly every politician sticks his hand into the barrel at one time or another, so nearly every federal agency rushes around trying to fill it up. Agencies tend to be run by people who believe fervently in their work, even if no one else does, and they long ago learned to use the pork-barrel phenomenon to advance that work, doling out plums to powerful congressmen in return for favorable action on their budget requests. Those with the biggest plums to offer—the armed services with their military bases and weapons and hardware contracts, the Corps of Engineers and the Bureau of Reclamation with their dams and canals, the Department of Transportation with its highway and airport grants and its coast guard installations—have the most success and command the most attention, but they are by no means alone. The Census Bureau has been found with lard on its hands, designing surveys it wished to run so that the information generated would be of particular value to certain strategically placed congressmen. The National Institute of Health and the National Science Foundation have been caught doing the same thing with their grant programs. Pork, in the form of pet projects desired by congressmen who have to pass on their program and budget requests, has been found prominently displayed in the budgets of the Fish and Wildlife Service, the Forest Service, and the National Park Service.

In the spring of 1979, one ham-hunting congressman turned up the barrel, and out poured, of all people, Robert L. Duffey, the chairman of the National Endowment for the Humanities, busily sending out lists of humanities grants that each congressman could expect to obtain for his district if he voted Duffey's fund requests into place. "And I guess that may appear a little shocking to people when done in the arts and humanities," Common Cause staff member Bruce Adams told me a few days later, "but it's merely an extension of the existing system. What Duffey's doing is what the system is. That's how you get your appropriations." It's also how you waste money, of course, but no one seems to care very much about such matters in the agencies, where the standard attitude is too often like the one which was once explained quite candidly by a Forest Service official at one of the endless congressional appropriations hearings: "Mr. Chairman, you would not think that it would be proper for me to be in charge of this work and not be enthusiastic about it and not think that I ought to have a lot more money, would you? I have been in it for thirty years, and I believe in it."

Up to this point, we have been talking principally about the waste caused by pork barreling. But waste is not the only, or even necessarily the most important, impact of pork barreling on the American way of government. There are many other problems whose causes are traceable in whole or in part to Congress's love affair with lard.

- The pork-barrel system figures heavily in the problem of congressional favoritism toward special interests, mainly because these special interests tend to contribute so heavily to a congressman's or senator's campaign that he is likely to equate district interests with those of the special-interest groups within the district.

- Pork also interferes with the orderly activities of the great federal agencies, juggling agency planning, overriding agency expertise, politicizing agency decisions, and in the process fostering layer upon layer of red tape as the agencies and Congress each try to take control of the situation by issuing more regulations.

- Pork promotes interdistrict and interstate rivalries where enlightened self-interest would call for unity; it jams the congressional calendar and the law books with unnecessary sectarian legislation, and it trips up decision making on nonpork issues, both through its promotion of decisions through horse trading instead of statesmanship and through the sheer physical weight of committee and floor activity which must be devoted to points of pork, time and energy therefore not available for pondering points of state.

- Pork has caused massive environmental damage: little things like drying up the Everglades, pouring saline-saturated waters into Mexico and Canada in violation of international treaties and in callous disregard of the complaints of the Mexican and Canadian governments, and filling in fifty-one valleys in Mississippi and Alabama with the soil dug from a canal being built at a cost to the taxpayers of $1.8 billion because a few barge companies have convinced a few powerful congressmen that the current barge route from the Kentucky coalfields to the Gulf of Mexico is too long. (The new canal, known as the Tennessee-Tombigbee—Tenn-Tom, for short—will cut barge time from Kentucky to the gulf by all of about fifty-six hours.)

These are some of the more obvious problems. Others are more subtle. In fact, one of these almost invisible effects is in many ways the worst of all. It is probably best illustrated by the fate of a piece of relatively recent legislation which on its face is one of the most successful pork-barrel reform bills ever to squeeze its way out of a reluctant Congress: a precedent-setting planning law called the Public Buildings Act of 1959.

The Public Buildings Act was a product of the seventh year of the Eisenhower Administration and of the fiscally conservative mood sweeping the country in those waning years of the cold war. After more than a century and a half of pork barreling with the construction of post offices and other federal buildings, the act's provisions seemed like a welcome and long-overdue breath of fresh air. Among other things, it reorganized the General Services Administration's Public Buildings Service, did away with the president's disastrous "lease-purchase" experiment in which private firms built public buildings and then leased them to the government at exorbitant rates on long-term options, and established tough new standards of need which any proposed federal building would henceforth have to meet.

Prior to this legislation, a new post office or other federal building had been one of the easiest and most dependable ways for a congressman to funnel government spending into his district. The prevailing attitude toward such activities was probably best summed up in a statement by Representative Clifton A. Woodrum of Virginia. He reminded his colleagues during floor debate on an omnibus public buildings appropriations bill in 1937 that there was "a general understanding that every member of the House will be provided for if his district has an eligible project." Just how loosely that eligibility was defined may be judged by some of the projects for which bills had been introduced that year. They included post offices and federal buildings for such thriving metropolises as Ada, Minnesota (population 1,938); Pe Ell, Washington (population 825); Barnwell, South Carolina (population 1,922); and Webster Springs, West Virginia (unincorporated; population unlisted). A decade and a half later, in 1951, a director of the Bureau

of the Budget reported to an amazed congressional committee that he had received requests for "eligible projects"
in their districts from more than two hundred congressmen
in one recent three-month period. The stringent needs
criteria of the Public Buildings Act were obviously long
overdue, and when the act was passed there was a collective
sigh of relief from antipork campaigners who were convinced that at least one major federal construction program
had now climbed out of the barrel and was standing on its
own two feet.

Did the new law, with all its good intentions, do its job?

In June 1979, twenty years after the Public Buildings Act
went into effect, I paid a call on the man responsible for
administering it, Acting General Services Administration
Chief Paul S. Goulding, a corpulent, soft-spoken ex-Senate
staffer who had stepped into what is perhaps the hottest
seat in Washington a few months before with the resigna-
tion under fire of Jay Solomon. "You have to have federal
employees to get federal buildings," Goulding assured me.
"If there's no agency need, then it's impossible. We have
congressmen all the time who write to us and say, 'I think
there may be a need for a new federal building in my home
town,' or some town in their district. We say, 'Fine, we'll
look into it.' We look into it, and we say, 'Well, we've got
four or five little agencies there, we've got a social security
office, we've got an army recruiting office, and IRS has a
taxpayers' assistance office, and the postal department has
a facility which isn't under our control, and VA has a facility
which isn't under our control, and—I'm sorry, we don't
need a new building for any purpose,' and we tell them so,
all the time. If there's no need, there's no building, and in
that sense there isn't any waste in the program.

"Now, what's happened, though, is that we've gotten
into a situation where the need exists almost everywhere,
and the question has become the *priority* of need. Right
now, for instance, we have a shortfall of over a million

square feet of space that we need to house federal agencies here in the District of Columbia. We've been negotiating leases with landowners, who know we don't have anywhere else to go, which puts us in a noncompetitive situation, and the escalation of lease costs is incredible. But at the same time, there's no new construction program, because the Office of Management and Budget has not approved a GSA request for a building program since December of 1974. So that really puts us at the mercy of Congress to pass whatever *they* deem to be new construction programs. We're working in a vacuum, not with a plan of our own, but dependent on the plans that Congress makes. And, speaking as someone who worked up there for sixteen years, why would any man or woman in his or her right mind sit on the Public Works Committee in the House or the Senate if they didn't have anything to say about where public works were going to be constructed? And I recognize their prerogatives, but that does not set priorities. We desperately need not one, but several new federal buildings in the District of Columbia area. The highest priority is right here, right now. But Washington, D.C., does not have a voting representative in Congress."

In one sense, then, the Public Buildings Act has clearly been a success. The taxpayers' money is not being wasted; federal buildings are not being built without a firm demonstration of need. But in another sense, the act is just as clearly a failure. For the pork-barrel system it sought to eliminate is still very much there—not wasting money, but now setting priorities.

This problem is not confined to the General Services Administration. In every agency, throughout every level of government, major priorities are continually being set by pork rather than by planning. With amazing regularity, defense contracts are awarded not to the firms most qualified to do the work, but to firms in the states of Armed Services Committee members; dams are built not where

dams are most desperately needed, but where they will
benefit the states of Public Works Committee members;
tariffs are set not according to an international strategy of
trade, but on the products manufactured in the states of
Commerce Committee members.

Worse yet, goals are chosen and broad courses of national action decided not on the basis of what is best for the
country but on the basis of what is best for certain states
or congressional districts. Is solar power better than nuclear? We'll never know as long as the energy committees
of Congress are dominated by members from states like
Washington (Hanford), New Mexico (Alamogordo) and
Tennessee (Oak Ridge). Are nonstructural means of flood
control better than dams? Not as long as dams cost more
and congressmen remain convinced that the only way to
get reelected is to pull huge amounts of federal money into
their districts. Are bombers a better means of national defense than battleships? The answer is yes to congressmen
whose states contain aircraft plants, no to those whose
states contain shipyards. Day after day, on decision after
decision, the congressional choices continue to be made
this way: not on whether something should be done but on
who should do it, not on where a new facility can be most
efficiently located but on which state or district can land
that particular federal-spending plum. Some examples:

- In the early 1960s, NASA needed to build a manned
  spaceflight center to coordinate communications on the
  Apollo Moon effort. There were several logical places
  where this center could have been located: at Cape Canav-
  eral itself, avoiding duplication of facilities; in Hawaii, to
  be close to the splashdown area; in Colorado Springs or
  in Alamogordo, sharing facilities and services with the Air
  Force Academy or the White Sands Proving Ground. It
  ended up in Houston—the home city of Albert Thomas,

chairman of the Appropriations Subcommittee dealing with the space program.

● In the mid-1970s, AMTRAK inaugurated a new passenger train from Washington to Cincinnati. Sources within the Transportation Department later admitted privately that their original plan had been to create a connection between Washington and Chicago, but that they had been derailed by West Virginia Congressman Harley O. Staggers, who insisted that the train go through his birthplace (Keyser, West Virginia), making the Chicago terminus no longer practical. "Who the hell," asked one transportation official rhetorically over a schooner of beer, "wants to go from Washington to Cincinnati?"

● In the spring of 1979, a battle royal was being fought in Congress over refurbishing the aircraft carrier S.S. *Saratoga*—not on the question of whether or not the refurbishment was economically or militarily desirable, but whether it should be done in Philadelphia or Newport News. "It's simple, and clear, and not a goddamn thing to do with national security," a Brookings Institution military specialist fumed to me, "except that presumably a refurbished aircraft carrier is better than a nonrefurbished one." Presumably: but as long as the question centers on who and not whether, we'll never know for sure.

All these are examples of minor priority rearrangements caused by pork barreling. But pork is active in major national priorities debates, too, shaping policy-making decisions at a level matched by few other single forces. Of the many areas of current policy debate where this principle can be demonstrated, perhaps the clearest, most confounding, and most infuriating examples are in the field of energy.

It is a major tenet of popular wisdom to blame the oil companies for the energy crisis, but it might be more to the point to blame Congress. Since the early 1950s, when a presidential commission appointed by Harry S. Truman first warned that the nation would run out of oil by the end of the century, congressional energy policy has been in the hands of committees run by men like Senator Robert Kerr, from oil-rich Oklahoma; Representative Wayne Aspinall, whose home state of Colorado contains huge deposits of uranium and oil shale; and Senator Henry M. Jackson of Washington, where the Hanford Atomic Energy Reservation houses the largest plutonium-production facility in the world. When President Jimmy Carter dropped his first national energy plan into Congress in 1977, it landed in the laps of a group of influential lawmakers that included Senator Russell B. Long, who came into the Senate on Louisiana oil money; Representative Mike McCormack, a former AEC scientist whose Washington district includes the Hanford Atomic Energy Reservation; Senator Robert C. Byrd, whose state of West Virginia is the nation's leading coal producer; Senator Ted Stevens of Alaska, who often acts as though the center of his state were in the Prudhoe Bay oil fields; and Representative Manuel Lujan of New Mexico, where the nuclear-oriented Energy Research and Development Administration spends more per capita than in any other state, 47 percent more than second-ranked Nevada and nearly three times as much as third-ranked Tennessee. There is little wonder that Carter's carefully crafted plan came out of Congress looking like fried spaghetti, riddled with loopholes and concessions for the oil, nuclear, and coal industries but with scarcely a nod toward such "nonporkable" items as solar power and conservation.

By the time he submitted his second plan, in the summer of 1979, Carter appeared to have learned his lesson; the new plan was built around synthetic fuels, an economically and environmentally disastrous technology which has been characterized as the "junk food of the energy industry" but

THE PORK-BARREL POLKA: 39

which is nevertheless highly porkable and therefore presumably attractive to Congress. Nonetheless, as of December 1979, the new plan looks to be in almost as much
trouble as the old, due mostly to the efforts of Senator
Long, whose devotion to the oil interests of his Louisiana
constituents would be touching if it weren't so damaging to
the rest of us.

The only real answer to America's energy woes lies in a
planned, rational conversion to renewable energy sources
such as the sun, combined with an aggressive conservation
program; but as long as congressional processes remain
bogged down in pork lard, there seems little chance that
any such unporkable program can make headway. So far,
the only spark of interest that Congress has shown in solar
power has been struck by the Solar Power Satellite (SPS)
program, a multibillion-dollar Buck Rogers scheme to
place up to sixty huge solar collectors in geosynchronous
orbit around the Earth. The electricity thus generated
would be beamed by microwave radiation to a few centrally
located antenna complexes, each of which would cover
some fifty square miles. The SPS program has been
severely criticized for lack of cost effectiveness, for questionable operational ability and for downright dangerous-
ness—critics have pointed out that the lethal nature of mi-
crowaves at the level required for transmission of
SPS-generated power would make the satellites convertible
into superbly effective weapons merely by retargeting the
energy beam. But the program would be a bonanza for the
aerospace industry, and it is therefore receiving strong congressional support from the delegations representing
southern California (Lockheed), New York (Grumman),
Maryland (Martin-Marietta), Connecticut (United) and
enough others so that the last SPS bill sailed through Congress by a vote of 267–96.

There have been occasional congressional voices raised
against the interference of pork in priority setting. In 1934,

Senator Oscar Underwood of Alabama complained that
". . . with great governmental issues at stake, I have been
compelled to accept minor amendments to great bills that
I will not say were graft, but they were put there for the
purpose of magnifying the importance of one man with his
constituency at the point of jeopardizing good legislation
in America." More recently, a California representative was
heard to complain after a series of district-specific votes
had been forced upon him that he had to ". . . continue
going this way and that, back and forth. I'm a cracker-ass
congressman, and I could have been a statesman." During
debate on the 1979 Public Works Appropriations bill, Congressman Bob Edgar of Pennsylvania chided his colleagues
for setting their spending priorities by pork barreling,
"thereby demonstrating once more that we may deserve
the low regard in which we are held by the American public.
. . . Here we are, before our public, lining up at the trough."

However, most congressmen defend the practice as a
proper approach to planning, usually on the basis that what
is best for the district is automatically best for the nation,
and that only the individual congressman knows what is
best for his own district. "The bureaucracy," remarked
New York Representative Benjamin A. Gilman recently of
an Office of Management and Budget attempt to impose priority standards on water projects, "does not have
that kind of direct responsibility to the people which is
invested in this body." "The bill we bring the members
today is truly an all-American bill," observed Indiana Representative John T. Myers admiringly the same day of a
public-works bill; ". . . there is not a congressional district
in this body that is not affected." Such statements, of
course, ignore what should be an obvious fact: one person's boon may be another's boondoggle. What is best for
one district may actually be harmful to the country as a
whole. A law requiring us all to smoke two packs of ciga-
rettes a day would certainly help the tobacco-growing

states, but it wouldn't do much for the rest of us. But the Gilmans, the Myers, and the great majority of the other 533 members of the House and Senate continue to insist that this form of reasoning is valid.

Bob Kerr, at least, was honest. As senator from Oklahoma in the 1950s and early 1960s, Kerr was one of the greatest pork-barrelers of all time, but he never pretended to be working for the benefit of anyone but his own constituents. Perhaps his most famous observation on the matter came during a debate with Senator Albert Gore of Tennessee in the late 1950s. Gore had taken the Senate floor to complain about tax loopholes which accrued large benefits to special interests such as the Oklahoma oil producers, and Kerr lit into him. "The senator from Tennessee speaks of tax loopholes," he observed sarcastically. "It does not particularly astonish me that in his list of supposedly unwholesome tax benefits he includes none of those advantages which inure to the benefit of Tennessee. Nor do I consider those which help to create jobs and a better climate of business in Oklahoma to be unwholesome. I think they are very wholesome. I do not think of them as loopholes. I think of them as properly conceived incentives and aids to the economy."

Bob Kerr is dead now, but his soul goes marching on.

2

The Pork Ethic

Anyone who doubts the wisdom of the old saw about power consisting of being in the right place at the right time should spend a little while examining the relation of federal spending in the various states to the committee structure of Congress. Almost universally, the lion's share of the spending of any federal agency ends up going to the states of the senators and representatives who are members of the committees which oversee the affairs of that particular agency. In 1976, for example, looking principally at the Senate:

- The average per-capita spending of the Department of the Interior for all fifty states was $43.81. In those states with senators on the Senate Interior Committee, however, the average per-capita spending jumped to $86.48, virtually twice the national average. And those states lucky enough to have a member on the Senate Appropriations Committee's Subcommittee on the Interior did even better. There the average per-capita spending was $99.97. Between them, the two committees managed to represent every one of the top ten states in per-capita Interior spending—three of them twice (Wyoming, Montana and Idaho).

- The Department of Agriculture spent $83.05 per capita in the average state. For those states with members on the Senate Agriculture Committee, the average was $95.64.
- The states of Senate Commerce Committee members received an average of $20.89 per capita in Department of Commerce funds; the average national per-capita figure was only $12.41.
- Per-capita spending by the Energy Research and Development Administration in those states with members on the Joint Committee on Atomic Energy was two and one-half times the national average, outstripping those states without committee members by a margin of $83.92 to $33.59.
- Those states with the good fortune to have someone on one of the four Senate committees dealing with the military could really rake in the bucks. In the nation as a whole, the Department of Defense spent an average of $448.27 per capita per state. But in the states of Armed Services Committee members, the average leaped up to $557.97; in the states of that committee's Subcommittee on Military Construction Authorization, defense spending averaged $614.93 per capita; in the states represented by members on the Senate Appropriations Committee's Subcommittee on Defense, the average edged upward another notch, to $629.39; and in those states with members on the Appropriations Committee's Subcommittee on Military Construction, it jumped to a whopping $738.33, almost $300 extra for every man, woman and child in the state. With the population of the average state now pegged at about 4.5 million, this meant that having a senator on the Military Construction Subcommittee was worth something in the neighborhood of $1.3 billion to the average state in Defense Department spending each and every year.

These figures provide one measure of how deeply the pork-barrel system is engrained in the congressional process. Another can be found in the lopsided vote by which most of these items pass the House and Senate, even in the face of clear evidence that they are worthless. The huge and costly water-manipulation schemes of the Army Corps of Engineers and the Bureau of Reclamation are particularly outstanding examples of this. Usually these projects are hustled through Congress on voice votes with such clearly defined differences in volume between the "ayes" and the "noes" that no one bothers to count, but occasionally some antipork congressman will get mad and demand a record vote.

In June 1979, one of these rare record votes took place on the Stonewall Jackson Dam, a $115 million West Virginia bauble which the Corps wants to build on the upper West Fork of the Monongahela River. Less worthwhile uses of $115 million would be hard to find. A detailed examination of the project's economics by specialists at the Environmental Policy Center in Washington led them to call it "one of the weakest economic justifications we have ever seen": they computed a benefit/cost ratio of 0.43 to 1, a return of just 43 cents for every tax dollar to be spent. Economics professor Thomas C. Campbell of West Virginia University concurred with the EPC analysis, noting that in his opinion the economics of Stonewall Jackson were "far too weak," leaving the project "not even close to being justified." Letters opposing the dam were filed with the Corps by West Virginia Agriculture Commissioner Gus Douglas, West Virginia Secretary of State A. James Manchin, the United Mine Workers, the American Farm Bureau Federation, the West Virginia Council of Churches and numerous other individuals and organizations. "That Stonewall Jackson Dam," fumed one congressman privately after the vote, "is good for absolutely nothing, except it will ruin a bunch of farmland, and that's about it."

But when Representative Bob Edgar of Pennsylvania brought all this out on the floor of the House, he might as well have been blowing into a hot-air balloon. Local businessmen were convinced that a dam would be good for the local economy, and what's good for the local economy is good for Congress. Stonewall Jackson boomed onto the budget by a vote of 96–13.

The lopsided vote on the Stonewall Jackson project and the lopsided patterns of spending by federal agencies in relation to the congressional committees that oversee them indicate clearly that pork is not a surface phenomonon. It is a deeply imbedded cog in the congressional decision-making process. It is extremely important to understand this point. Pork barreling is not an act of rule breaking engaged in by a few venal congressmen for personal or political gain, nor is it a set of loopholes in the legislative system which Congress has purposefully set up to exploit to its own advantage. It is a mainline activity, one of the two or three principal methods by which Congress transacts the governmental business of the United States of America. Pork barreling is the rule rather than the exception; far from being a violation of congressional standards, it is the base upon which those standards are built. Congress is in the grip of what must be called, for better or worse, the pork ethic, and where that ethic leads, the rest of legislation must follow.

That this should be so derives not from some nefarious plot by the Founding Fathers, but from a fundamental— and probably unavoidable—flaw in America's representational system of government. This flaw, simply put, is that the system *is* representational. Every senator, and every member of the House, comes to the federal legislature as a delegate from a geographically discrete political unit. Senators represent individual states; members of the House represent individual congressional districts. To *represent,* according to *Funk & Wagnall's Standard Desk Dictio-*

nary, is to "serve as or be the delegate, agent, etc., of." An *agent,* according to the same source, is "one who acts for or by the authority" of another. Senators and members of the House act for and by the authority of the states and districts that elect them, and their first duty is therefore to those states and districts, rather than to the nation as a whole. On issues that are wholly or largely ideological in nature—war and peace, crime and punishment, civil rights and civil liberties—the system works splendidly, because the interests of the nation as a whole and the interests of the various parts that go to make up that whole coincide, and discharging one's duties to one's constituents involves merely the exercise of good judgment. The ideology of the laws thus reflects the ideology of the nation, and that is as it should be.

Unfortunately, however, most problems which face the federal government are not ideological in nature. Instead, they are *distributive*—they involve not what should be done, but who gets how much of something—like money, or highways, or military contracts, or canals, or railroad service. And here the system breaks down. Because now one's duty to one's constituents is not to use one's judgment on their behalf but to get something for them, not to decide what kind of cake to put on the plate but to grab the biggest hunk possible when it comes around. Constituent duties and the pork ethic become synonymous.

Am I being overly pessimistic? Perhaps, but I am not alone. Recall the previously quoted remark of Congressman Jim Wright of Texas: "One major facet of a congressman's duties is that of providing desirable results for his own district." Since Wright was subsequently elected House majority leader, someone must agree with what he is saying. One who clearly does is Wright's counterpart on the other side of Capitol Hill, Senate Majority Leader Robert C. Byrd. "I tell my constituents they've got five friends," the folksy, fiddle-playing West Virginian allowed to reporters not long ago. "God, Sears Roebuck, Montgomery Ward, Carter's Pills, and Robert C. Byrd."

In a more serious and scholarly vein, political scientists Jack Plano and Milton Greenburg argue in their *American Political Dictionary* that the problem of pork barreling "basically . . . relates to the theory of representation. The American representative goes to his legislature or to Congress as the representative of the people of his district rather than of the state or nation. This means that he will be expected by his constituents to perform creditably on their behalf." And at the Brookings Institution, Washington's prestigious, privately endowed center for the study of American government, senior research fellow Joel Aberbach concurs. "In American politics, the attempt has traditionally been to turn every issue into a matter of distribution," Aberbach told me. "Take something that was very controversial fifteen years ago—federal education grants. That is much less controversial now. And it's much less controversial because it's turned from a great ideological issue about what role the federal government ought to play in education, or *whether* it ought to play a role, to a question of the distribution of benefits to all the districts around the country through various types of education grants. Some congressmen are still opposed to the current education policies, but many of them, it turns out, have people in their districts who want something. So in that sense, the thing gets going, and it's very hard to stop." The pork ethic takes over, and the barrel just gets bigger and bigger.

Read over in the cold, clear light of the morning after writing them, the words of the above passage seem to imply quite strongly that there is something inherently wrong with constituent services and with the whole process of Congress acting as a distribution agency. This, I must hasten to point out, is not true. Most of what falls under the heading of constituent services is quite remote from any-

thing that could be considered pork barreling. It includes
such things as acting as ombudsman for citizens who are
having trouble with the red-tape wielders who so often
seem to represent the great federal agencies on the local
level, or helping someone from their district who has trav-
eled to Rwanda and then lost passport, visa, ticket, or all
three, or submitting military-academy nominations to the
president on behalf of local youths, or even helping someone from back home find hotel space and a place to cash
his traveler's checks in Washington. And the distributive
function—Congress as resource allocator—is equally valid,
at least in concept. Indeed, you might ask yourself whom
you would rather have dictating where your taxes are to be
spent. The president? The Internal Revenue Service?
Agency bureaucrats? It wasn't so long ago that Americans
fought a revolution over taxation without representation,
after all; and it wasn't representation in the decisions concerning how much to tax that was the principal point of
contention, but representation in the councils that decided
where the money was to go. The writers of the Constitution
had just been through that quarrel, and they knew what
they were doing when they put the purse strings in the
hands of the newly created United States Congress. It is
neither the distributive function of Congress, nor constituent services, that is wrong; what is wrong is that they tend
to get confused with each other.

A congressman who is properly discharging his constituent duties is making sure that citizens with complaints are
not overlooked by the government, and that is good. A
congressman who is properly discharging his distributive
function is making sure that areas with needs are not overlooked by the government, and that is also good. But a
congressman who confuses the two is confusing citizens
with areas and complaints with needs, and that is not so
good. By themselves, constituent duties and the distributive function serve admirably to bring to life that eloquent

phrase of the Declaration of Independence which reminds us that "all men are created equal"; confused with each other, they interpret the Declaration along the lines of George Orwell's *Animal Farm:* "All men are created equal, but some are more equal than others." Congress manages to confuse them all the time.

Perhaps the most ludicrous, and at the same time the most revealing, example of the ends to which this "some are more equal than others" confusion can lead is the case of Congressman Will Whittington and the Mississippi River. The story is more than thirty years old, now, but it still bears repeating. Whittington was a small-town lawyer from Mississippi who represented his district in the House of Representatives for twenty-six years, beginning in 1925 and ending with the opening of the Eighty-second Congress in January 1951. For the last two years of this period he was chairman of the House Public Works Committee; for many years before that he chaired that committee's Subcommittee on Flood Control. These chairmanships gave him considerable power over water resource development, power which he used to gain a rather unusual advantage over his neighbors across the river in Louisiana, where Senator Allen Ellender was still fuming over it many years later. "He always saw to it," complained Ellender, "that the levees on the Mississippi side were about three feet higher than the ones on the Louisiana side, so that Louisiana would get flooded before Mississippi would."

This, of course, is district favoritism taken to extremes, and one is tempted to dismiss it as a mere aberration—until one realizes the context in which Ellender made the remark. The scene was the 1966 Senate hearings on the forthcoming rivers and harbors appropriations for fiscal year 1967; Ellender was siding with Senator Paul Douglas of Illinois as he attempted to head off precisely the same sort of levee development on the Wabash. The Indiana delegation had been busily pushing levees through on their

side and watching the water pour out all over Senator
Douglas's people in Illinois. Nearly twenty years had
passed, but the spirit of Will Whittington was alive and
well. It still is.

Congressmen tend to take the pork ethic extremely seriously. One measure of this is the way in which it shows up
so frequently in election-year advertising, disguised as a
campaign slogan. Some recent examples, chosen randomly
from Arnold Fochs's titillating collection, *Advertising That
Won Elections:*

- Representative Richardson Preyer, telling the voters in
  his North Carolina district that "Rich Preyer Works for
  You."
- Representative Charles E. Chamberlain, booming himself
  to the voters in his Michigan district as "Your Man in
  Washington."
- Senator James O. Eastland, letting Mississippians know
  that "When there's a job to be done for Mississippi, Jim
  Eastland is there."
- Representative John A. Blatnik of Minnesota, reminding
  voters that "If something needs to be done for the 8th
  district . . . Blatnik" will do it.
- Representative Charles Thone of Nebraska proclaiming
  that "Charley Thone is a man at work . . . important work
  for Nebraskans."
- Senator Gordon Allott of Colorado, publishing a long list
  of his successful forays to the pork barrel on behalf of his
  state—Department of Transportation research facilities,
  Bureau of Reclamation dams, Corps of Engineers levees
  —and concluding that he should be reelected "For the
  Future of Colorado and Her People."

Another measure of the pork ethic's dominance lies in
the amount of space given to touting works won for the
district in the pages of those newsy little fact sheets that
congressmen regularly send out, over their frank, to every

street address and post-office box in their district. Still another can be found in the amount of time congressmen devote to what is loosely called "constituent duties," a category which claims between one-fourth and one-third of a congressman's own time and roughly half the time of his staff.

And there are also the pages of the *Congressional Record,* where transcripts of floor debate reveal startlingly high proportions of the time that Congress should be spending discussing the issues devoted instead to long-winded speeches on district-specific items that members of the House and Senate want their colleagues to approve for them. This is particularly true during debate on the great appropriations bills. I have before me, for example, a partial record of the floor debate on 1979's H.R. 4388, the Energy and Water Development Appropriations for 1980. This debate ran to 47 pages—141 columns—of small print in the *Record.* Eighteen of those pages were ideological, devoted to impassioned debate on whether or not intervenors in federal regulatory cases should have their expenses offset by federal appropriations. The remaining twenty-nine were distributive, of which fourteen pages—nearly half—were devoted either to flowery praise of committee members for having included specific projects in the praiser's district, or to defense of the bill against specific project cuts, primarily by those whose districts would be affected by the cuts. (Because congressmen have the right to "revise and extend" their remarks in the *Record*—that is, to take out those passages which they wish they hadn't said and put in the stuff they wanted to say but forgot about in the heat of the moment—the *Record* is often disparaged as an accurate source concerning what *really* went on in the House or Senate. However, I was present in the gallery for most of this particular debate, and the *Record*'s account seems reasonably accurate. Besides, congressmen probably delete remarks about pork as often as they place them in. I am reminded of the story of John Nance Garner of Texas, who, as Speaker of the House, once remarked in the heat of debate, "Every time those damn Yankees get a hambone, I'm going to get a hog." No trace of this clear admission of pork barreling appeared in the *Record* the next day.)

So the pork ethic is very deeply felt, and the commitment to it on the part of virtually every member of Congress is extremely strong. But this raises a question: what happens when this deeply felt and strongly committed ethic comes into conflict with other congressional ethics which may also be deeply felt and strongly committed? What happens when pork conflicts with a member's stand as a dove or a hawk, as a federalist or a states righter, as a big spender or a fiscal conservative? What happens, in short, when the hand that reaches into the pork barrel must first pass through a circle of ideological fire?

At the Brookings Institution in Washington, I discussed this issue with Senior Fellow Thomas A. Dine, a specialist in defense and foreign policy whose current project is following the SALT II debates. ("I'm writing a monograph on SALT III," he told me, shortly after we met. "It's called 'Optimism.'") Tom Dine knows his way around on the Hill; before coming to the Brookings he served as a Senate staff member in various capacities for nine years; before that he served as director of congressional liaison for the Peace Corps. He put the issue of pork vs. ideology to me in the form of a rhetorical question: "When," he asked, "is a guy the United States senator from New York—and when is he the New York senator? Throughout his day, that changes back and forth, and you never know for sure how it's going to come out. And the wider the gap, obviously the more it tears a guy up, because of the contradictions facing him minute after minute.

"Take Carter's Korean troop-withdrawal policy, for example. When that was announced in the spring of '77, a guy like Pat Moynihan just went bananas. That was not his definition of national security. Leave 'em in there, and show those North Koreans, and those other commies, that we're tough, and—I dare Premier Kim to send his troops across the thirty-eighth parallel. Aha! But then, as this began to form and to shape as national policy, the New York delegation, including Senator Moynihan, began to talk about, well, if you're going to take a division out of Korea, where are you going to *put* it? Ah—Fort Drum, in Waterville, New York! Jesus Christ, we've got to make sure it happens at Fort Drum! So all of a sudden, the junior senator from New York began working to make sure that that contingent, if it *did* come out of Korea, was going to come to *his* backyard, and not somebody else's.

"So. When was the junior senator from New York acting in the national interest, and when was he acting in the local interest? When was he the senator from New York, and when was he the New York senator? And these things play back and forth constantly."

Many other examples could be cited. Back in the late 1940s, for example, Representative L. Mendel Rivers of South Carolina, one of the great congressional conservatives, stepped briefly out of character to lead a massive and successful consumer-advocacy fight against restrictions on the sale of colored margarine; a role reversal which appears much less quixotic when you realize that Rivers's district was one of the nation's major producers of cottonseed oil, an important margarine ingredient. Rivers, whose perennial campaign slogan was "Rivers Delivers," was merely delivering for another constituent interest. Similarly, in 1974, Idaho's solidly right-wing Senator James L. McClure had a brief fling at being an environmentalist, taking an active leading role in the Senate fight in favor of a massive land lockup and resource freeze around Hells Canyon in the western part of his state. He had taken a survey of Idaho voters and found them in favor of a Hells Canyon National

Recreation Area by better than two to one, and that made
the issue a rather attractive piece of pork.

On the other hand, Arizona's liberal Congressman Mor-
ris Udall, who usually votes with environmentalists, almost
always votes against them when it comes to water projects.
Arizona is a dry state, and Udall clearly feels that a vote
against water projects will be construed back home as a
vote against the district. And Congressman Bob Edgar of
Pennsylvania, whose proenvironment voting record is virtually spotless, voted against the environmentalists on the
key mass-transit/highway trust fund issue in 1978. Why?
The League of Conservation Voters' answer is probably as
good as anyone's: "A few of our usual friends," they noted
in their analysis of this vote, "went the other way because
of their need to repair bridges in their districts."

The best example of the pork ethic overriding ideology,
though, is probably the case of Senator Ted Stevens of
Alaska reacting to issues raised by the National Environmental Policy Act and the Alaska Pipeline. The National
Environmental Policy Act, usually known by its acronym,
NEPA, declares it the policy of the United States government to take the environment into account in all major
decisions. Certain specific means of enforcing this policy
are spelled out, including the filing of environmental impact statements and the serious consideration of possible
alternative courses of action whenever a federal agency is
about to embark on an action whose impact on the environment is potentially severe. With its bold, sweeping statement of purpose ("To declare a national policy which will
encourage productive and enjoyable harmony between
man and his environment; to promote efforts which will
prevent or eliminate damage to the environment and bio-
sphere and stimulate the health and welfare of man; to
enrich the understanding of the ecological systems and
natural resources important to the Nation"), NEPA does
not merely conform to environmentalist ideology, it

defines it. The act and the ideology are virtually synonymous, and its sponsors must therefore be considered its
ideologues. There were two of these sponsors in the Senate
when the act passed in the summer of 1969; one was Senator Stevens.

Three years later, in the summer of 1971, the Senate
found itself embroiled in a major controversy over the best
means to move the products of Alaska's rich North Slope
oil fields to the population centers of the other forty-nine
states of the union. At issue were two possible pipeline
routes, one largely through Canada, the other entirely
within the boundaries of Senator Stevens's state. Of the
two, the Canadian route seemed clearly preferable, both on
environmental and economic grounds. It would cross fewer
sensitive areas, disrupt fewer wildlife-migration patterns,
require no ocean transport, and deliver the oil to the Midwest, where it was needed, rather than to the Pacific Coast,
where it was not. (The importance of this last point was
drilled home in the summer of 1979 when a second major
pipeline controversy erupted, this time over the so-called
Northern Tier Pipeline, designed to transport Alaska crude
from West Coast ports to Chicago. There is no need to go
into the complex pros and cons of this Northern Tier route
to make the point that this particular brouhaha was, or
should have been, totally needless. If they'd built the damn
thing right in the first place, the oil would already be going
to Chicago.) Unfortunately, the Canadian route would have
given far fewer immediate benefits to Senator Stevens's
home state; and the Senate, always alert to its members'
pork-barrel needs, indicated clearly that it intended to pass
legislation authorizing the Alaska route. Environmentalists
sued, using the senator's own farseeing NEPA legislation,
and won a ruling that the Canadian alternative had not
been properly considered. However, it was a Pyrrhic victory. Almost immediately the Senate passed legislation, not
authorizing adequate consideration of the Canadian route,

but *exempting the pipeline from NEPA review.* And one of the
prime sponsors of this new law weakening Senator Stevens's National Environmental Policy Act was Senator Stevens.

Along with the excellent example it presents of the dominance of pork over ideology at most points where the two
come into conflict, the case of Senator Stevens and the
Alaska Pipeline also affords us a brief look at a facet of the
pork ethic which we will be delving into in considerably
greater detail later—the role played by monied special interests in the pork-barrel system. One of the classic money-
bags/capitalist bogeymen of our time, "Big Oil," obviously
had a great deal to gain from the construction of the pipeline, and its presence on Capitol Hill during the pipeline
debates was not small. Does this mean that the Senate in
general, and Senator Stevens in particular, was in the
pocket of Big Oil when the decision was made? Is Congress, as has so often been charged, a prisoner of the lobbies and the special interests?
It is not possible to give an unequivocal answer to that
question for the Alaska Pipeline without going into the
subject in considerably more depth than I am prepared to
at the moment, but it seems highly unlikely. And for the
general run of pork-barrel issues confronting Congress,
the answer is clearly no. Though there are lapses—the cele-
brated Tongsun Park "Koreagate" scandals of the late
1970s provide an excellent case in point—influence ped-
dling on the Hill is actually quite a rare event, and what
passes for special-interest favoritism almost always turns
out, when examined closely, to be a case of district favoritism instead. Though it might be possible to say that Senator Stevens was in the pocket of Big Oil during the pipeline
debates, it would be much more to the point to say that he
was in the pocket of Alaska.
This is not to say that the lobbies do not play an impor-

tant role in the pork-barrel system; they do, and we will be examining that role in some detail later in this book. The question is not whether the lobbies wield power, but whence that power derives. Conventional wisdom suggests that it derives from campaign slush funds, catered luncheons, Caribbean cruises and other symptoms of an unholy alliance between congressmen and lobbyists; evidence suggests, however, that it derives from the pork ethic.

Consider the position in which Senator Stevens found himself. When the oil companies first began discussing plans for the pipeline in 1969, its cost had been estimated at $900 million. That cost had almost immediately started blooming upward as they redesigned the line to handle more flow and as they discovered some of the extraordinary construction problems along the line's 789-mile path. By 1973, when the crucial Senate vote exempting the pipeline from NEPA review came along, unofficial cost estimates had risen into the multibillion dollar range (the Alyeska Pipeline Company's official estimate the next spring, when they began work, was $6 billion; the final cost was closer to $12 billion).

At the same time, the total annual personal income of Alaska citizens—the cumulative sum of money earned by every man, woman and child in the state in one year's time —was $3.5 billion. Even at the low-end estimate, therefore, the cost of the pipeline was more than one-fourth the total annual earning power of the state's citizens; if the costs went up as expected, they might end up as high as two to four times that total earning power. If the line were built totally within Alaska, the state would get the lion's share of that money; if the Canadian route were chosen, Canada would come up with most of it. There were also the port facilities that would be built at Valdez, Alaska (unnecessary if the pipeline went to Chicago) and the little matter of the state's 12.5 percent royalty on the wellhead price of the oil, which stood to shrink considerably if the pipeline went through Canada. The federal government was setting that wellhead price on the basis of a complicated formula which took into account transportation costs along the pipeline: the higher the transport costs, the lower the wellhead price. The Canadian route was longer and subject to Canadian tariffs, and would almost certainly raise that transport price by a significant amount. Calculations based on the expected flow rate of the oil had indicated that every penny the transportation costs went up would lower the state of Alaska's royalties by a cool million dollars per day. With all those facts staring him in the face, Senator Stevens really had no choice. There was no need for Big Oil to talk him into the Alaska route; on the contrary, it seems hardly likely that they could have talked him out of it.

The same principle clearly holds true for other pork-barrel projects. When Senator Henry M. Jackson, for instance, wangles another multimillion-dollar contract for Boeing, it is not entirely fair to call him the "senator from Boeing," as his critics so often do. Since Boeing is Seattle's largest employer, and Seattle is Washington's largest city, the pork ethic is at least as important as the Boeing connection. When a representative presses for a gigantic flood-control dam in his district instead of opting for more efficient and less destructive nonstructural flood-control methods such as flood-plain zoning, he is not necessarily on the payroll of the local heavy-construction workers' union. A dam will pump far more federal money into the district than will ever be forthcoming from a flood-plain land-use plan, and while all the other 434 congressional districts in the nation will have to supply a share of that dam money, his constituents will get all the benefits from it. When Representative James L. Oberstar of Minnesota advocates a billion-dollar winter navigation program for the St. Lawrence Seaway whose principal beneficiary will be U.S. Steel, don't waste your time looking for connections between that advocacy and the size of U.S. Steel's contribu-

tion to Oberstar's campaign fund. The relevant figure is the
number of Oberstar's constituents that the steel company
employs. The key here again is the pork ethic, and Oberstar's need to appear effective to the voters so that they will
send him back for two more years.

Common Cause, the national "citizens' lobby" founded
in 1970 by former presidential cabinet member John W.
Gardner, has developed a concept which expresses this
nicely. America, it charges, has become a "special-interest
state," a government dominated by what Common Cause's
president, David Cohen, has called "the power of special-
interest groups to influence government decisions in which
they have a major economic stake." The fuel for this
power? CC staff member Jane Wishner expressed it well in
a recent conversation in the organization's Washington
office. "Congress itself is a special-interest group," she told
me. "Their special interest lies in getting reelected, and the
benefits to them from these projects are politically in terms
of their local constituents." And Wishner's words find an
echo in two cogent sentences written more than a decade
previously by one of Congress's own, former Mississippi
Representative Frank E. Smith: "All members of Congress
have a primary interest in being reelected. Some members
have no other interest."

The pork ethic does not dominate entirely, of course.
Most members of Congress place the ideal of vote-by-con-
science ahead of the practical vote-by-expedience, at least
theoretically. They have elevated one who clearly did so—
Congresswoman Jeanette Rankin of Montana, the lone
congressional vote against United States entry into both
world wars—into the status of an in-House folk hero, and
they like to think that they live up to her example much of
the time. They disparage those who do not. The great
"Speaker Sam" Rayburn of Texas, Speaker of the House
for seventeen years prior to his death in 1961, was once

overheard remarking scornfully of such a member that he was "afraid of his district." A century or so earlier the same imagery had been used by President-to-be James A. Garfield; as a congressman, he wrote in the privacy of his journal (February 19, 1872) that it was "a terrible thing to live in fear of their constituents to the extent which many members do. I would rather be defeated every day in the year than suffer such fear." But the gap between ideal and real remains huge, and the congressman who does not pork most of the time, much as he may be admired, seldom feels as though he gets very far. Perhaps the best demonstration of this comes from the lips of Speaker Sam himself, in the form of an aphoristic bit of advice he used to give freshman legislators. "You want to get along?" the Speaker would ask. "Then go along."

3
The Congress Barrel

On May 22, 1979, veteran United States Senator Warren G. Magnuson stood up on the Senate floor and asked his colleagues to authorize an Army Corps of Engineers channel-improvement project for the port of Grays Harbor in his home state of Washington. "Grays Harbor," the senator was quoted in the *Congressional Record*, "has historically been one of our leading West Coast ports. Improved navigation facilities, as provided in this legislation, would result in maritime commerce continuing to develop on Grays Harbor. . . . The economic growth of the Far East market has generally expanded. The economic potentials of the Grays Harbor area have been held back by navigation limitations. . . . I hope, therefore, that the Public Works Committee will find this legislation acceptable." No costs were mentioned, but it was later revealed that the price tag for the Grays Harbor improvements would be a cool $59 million.

In any reasonable world, Magnuson's concern about the acceptability of this legislation would be fairly firmly grounded. For one thing, Grays Harbor is far from the "leading West Coast port" of which the senator had painted such a rosy picture; tonnage figures published by the Corps of Engineers reveal it as only the eighth busiest harbor in the state of Washington (never mind Alaska, California, and Oregon). For another, the Corps had already spent some $50 million for improvements to Grays Harbor in recent years while watching the population of the area's two principal cities, Aberdeen and Hoquiam, slide gradually and gracefully downhill from a combined total of 29,681 in 1940 to 28,700 in 1970. There was no indication that throwing another $59 million in that direction was going to be able to do anything the first $50 million hadn't. Finally, the federal Office of Management and Budget —the president's fiscal watchdog—had expressed strong misgivings about the project's design, noting that the Corps planned to create channels with dimensions "substantially greater than those required for safe navigation at Grays Harbor" and that the plan as a whole had many components which "appear to exceed traditional Corps of Engineers design standards." OMB had, in fact, requested that the plan not be submitted to Congress until these questions could be resolved (Magnuson complained that this would "only result in further duplication and delay"). In the topsy-turvy world of pork-barrel politics, however, none of this mattered very much. To most senators, the merits of the Grays Harbor legislation would not be nearly as important as the fact that Senator Magnuson is the current chairman of the Senate Appropriations Committee. With that going for it, the bill would be a shoe-in.

Congress is the center of power in the American federal system, a situation which is at once our greatest strength and one of our greatest weaknesses. The three traditional branches of power—legislative, executive, and judicial— which civics teachers are so fond of emphasizing, are separate but not equal. The power of the judiciary is limited to the negative task of telling Congress what it cannot do, not what it can, and it may only do this within very narrow constitutional limits. The president is similarly constrained: he cannot make laws, he can only enforce them, and his power even to do *that* is severely restricted by whether or not Congress chooses to give him the money to do it with. The massive bureaucratic apparatus of the great federal agencies, nominally a part of the executive branch and answerable only to the president, is actually bound to Congress so tightly by the twin strands of legislatively mandated programs and budgetary dependance that it constitutes a sort of political *coitus captivus.* Some critics maintain that this relationship has developed so far that certain agencies (notably the Corps of Engineers) have crossed the thin line between dependency and possession and become agencies of Congress rather than the president.

By putting them in the hands of elected representatives, the drafters of the Constitution guaranteed that these awesome powers would remain accountable to the citizenry; by apportioning those representatives to limited individual constituencies, they guaranteed that this accountability would develop along the lines of limited individual preferences. This is another way of saying that they built the pork ethic into the system. There are signs that Congress recognized this problem, and the sectional squabbling that would result from it, from the beginning. The first thing that the House of Representatives did after convening in New York City on March 4, 1789, was to delegate a committee to draw up rules for conducting legislative business without allowing the whole process to degenerate into a gigantic sectarian free-for-all.

The rules have been growing ever since. Today they have evolved into a complex and arcane jumble of points of order, social regulations, tests of germaneness, and so many other subtly shaded varieties of parliamentary gamesmanship that Congress long ago gave up even the pretense of being able to understand them on its own and hired someone to do it for them. Several someones, as a matter of fact. The Senate employs four full-time parliamentarians; the House has three, plus a legal assistant, clerk, and secretary. These ten people have collectively one of the toughest jobs in politics—the overwhelming, almost impossible chore of explaining Congress to itself.

But though the task seems Herculean (not too dissimilar from shoveling out the Augean stables), it is still possible for an outsider to make at least a small amount of sense out of it. There are several ways in which congressional procedures may be conceptualized. One way is to think of them as a gauntlet through which a bill must pass while its enemies—individual congressmen, groups of congressmen in the form of committees, and finally the entire membership of each house—flail at it with copies of *Robert's Rules of Order* and other lethal weapons. Those bills which succeed in running the gauntlet without getting clubbed to death become laws. A second possible model is that of a chess game in which the bill's sponsors develop a strategy within a clearly defined body of rules to move the bill square by square from the pawn row to the opponents' back row, where it becomes a queen. Yet a third analogy is that of the dance: the bill as ballerina, moving through an intricate series of prearranged steps which, if well performed, will earn applause in the form of floor votes and a presidential signature. But for our purposes, the best way to think about congressional structure is to look at it as simply a very large sieve.

Each year anywhere from sixteen to twenty thousand bills are introduced in Congress, four to five thousand in the Senate, and about three times that number in the House. Between three and four hundred of these bills will eventually become law; the remaining 15,500 or more will fall out along the way. In order to process this staggering number of bills without bogging down in procedure, and to maintain that necessary 98 percent attrition rate without either passing too many bad bills or throwing out too many good ones, Congress needs an efficient means of sifting the stream of legislation, letting the good bills through while catching and discarding the bad. The procedural sieve—or sieves, for there are actually thirty-six of them, thirty-six separate steps between a law's conception and its enactment—provides the means for achieving this sifting.

The odyssey of a bill through the maze of procedural sieves which constitutes the committee and subcommittee structure of the House and Senate begins with the hopper, a large square box on the desk of the presiding officer of each body. A senator or representative who wishes to introduce a bill has a printed copy made and literally "puts it in the hopper"—places it in that large square box. (He may also make an introductory speech on the floor, but this is a strictly superfluous bit of grandstanding for the folks back home. Thus it has been since earliest times. In fact, the dazzling lack of content in these introductory speeches has given rise to a widely used piece of American slang. In 1820, Felix Walker, a representative from Buncombe County, North Carolina, got up to give a speech on the House floor close to dinnertime. There were cries of distress from his hungry colleagues. Walker waved a hand at them expansively. "You can leave if you like," he said genially. "This is for Buncombe." These four words soon became the standard formula for any representative to use when he wanted to warn the other House members that what was to follow was strictly a pork speech, designed to catch the eyes of his constituents when printed in the district papers. From this practice have come our words *bunkum* and *bunk,* meaning empty nonsense. Introductory speeches are still Buncombe, and few in the chamber bother listening. Their crack at the bill will come later.)

The second step in the process involves the presiding officer (the Speaker of the House or the president of the Senate) and his staff, who sort through each day's crop from the hopper and refer bills to the proper committees. Technically, the presiding officer can kill a bill at this stage simply by refusing to refer it, but this power is seldom exercised. Almost all bills will reach the committee level, where they will be assigned by the committee chairman to one of his committee's six or seven subcommittees. It is at this point that the filtration begins in earnest.

The committee is the basic unit of the congressional filtration system. It is a small, clubby group of between fifteen and fifty representatives or senators (or occasionally, in the case of joint committees, both) with a task which is simple to define but profoundly difficult to carry out. It takes each bill assigned to it and decides, in as expeditious a manner as possible, whether to (a) submit it to the full membership of the House or Senate for a vote as written, (b) alter some of its provisions and submit the altered form for a vote of the full membership or (c) dump it altogether. In the early days of the republic, the Speaker of the House and the president of the Senate created a separate committee for each bill. But this soon grew cumbersome and was phased out in favor of so-called standing committees— groups with a fixed membership which take responsibility for all bills falling within a certain limited policy area (war and peace, foreign affairs, commerce, etc.). This system was already well codified by the time Henry Clay assumed the House speakership in 1811, and Clay put the finishing touches on it. Though the number, size and relative importance of the various committees have swung back and forth considerably since then, the essential nature of the committee structure has remained unchanged.

Currently the House has twenty-two standing committees; the Senate has fifteen. These numbers are set by statute, a limitation intended to control the problem of overlapping memberships and overlapping jurisdictions among committees that had practically paralyzed the government in the first half of this century. As usual, however, when it slammed the front door (via the Legislative Reorganization Act of 1946), Congress left the back door open. Along with the strictly limited number of standing committees, each house was given permission to set up virtually unlimited numbers of so-called "select" committees to function as task forces on specific problems and to go out of existence as soon as the problem is solved. Some, like the committees set up to probe the Watergate affair, do just that. Others do not. As of late 1979, the House and the Senate each had five select committees which showed signs of becoming permanently selected; one on the House side was in fact labeled a "permanent select committee." This brings the total number of Senate committees to twenty and the total in the House to twenty-seven.

Because both standing and select committees normally cover rather broad, general areas of policy—Commerce, Science, and Transportation, for example, or Banking, Housing, and Urban Affairs, or Environment and Public Works—they usually fine-tune themselves by breaking down still further into subcommittees. These are small, flexible groups of anywhere from three to two dozen members, each of which is charged with overseeing specific points of policy within the broad general jurisdiction of the parent committee. The Senate Committee on Environment and Public Works, for example, has subcommittees on Environmental Pollution, Nuclear Regulation, Regional and Community Development, Resource Protection, Transportation, and Water Resources. The House Committee on Education and Labor has subcommittees on Elementary, Secondary, and Vocational Education; Employment Opportunities; Health and Safety; Human Resources; Labor-Management Relations; Labor Standards; Postsecondary Education; and Select Education. And so forth. (The House Budget Committee calls its subcommittees "task forces," because the legislation which set it up, the Con-

gressional Budget Act of 1976, states quite specifically that
it is not to have any subcommittees. Which just goes to
show that where there's a will, there's a way.)

It is in these subcommittees that the principal work of the
committees—and hence of Congress—gets done: the crafting of bills, hearings on them, much of the amending, and
a good deal of the decision making as to whether a bill
should see further action or be quietly disposed of. In our
sieve analogy, the subcommittees can be thought of as an
entry screen, a first-level filter which receives the full force
of the legislative flood and passes on a much smaller stream
of relatively purified bills to be dealt with by the rest of the
system. There are 158 subcommittees in the House and
101 in the Senate, and they are very efficient. Of the more
than 15,500 bills killed in Congress each year, the overwhelming majority simply never get out of subcommittee.

A subcommittee's first step in dealing with those bills
that it decides are worth pursuing is normally to hold a
hearing—a quasi-judicial review during which the bill's
sponsor tells the subcommittee why he wants the bill
passed. Various other witnesses (agency officials, affected
citizens, other members of Congress) may also appear to
give their opinions. If no support for the bill is forthcoming
at the hearing, nothing else is likely to happen. But if support is there—and it usually is, or the hearing wouldn't
have been called in the first place—the bill will almost
certainly reach the next stage, a process known as the
markup. During a markup session, the members of the
subcommittee sit around a table and literally "mark up" the
bill, striking offending clauses and sections, changing others, perhaps adding a section or two, and occasionally
changing things so much that the bill's sponsor is forced to
repudiate it when it gets to the floor. Each change is approved by a vote of those present before it becomes official,
and at the end of the markup session a final vote is held on
the bill as a whole, as amended by the subcommittee. If the

bill fails here it dies; if it passes, it is said to be "reported out of subcommittee." The next move is to the full committee.

Full committee action on a bill is similar to subcommittee action without the hearings—it is all markup. Sometimes these full committee markup sessions are perfunctory, but more likely the bill will be further amended, with more clauses altered, deleted, and added. If the subcommittee was hostile to the bill and the full committee is less so, these changes may simply put the bill back the way it was before the subcommittee got hold of it.

At the end of the full committee markup there is another vote, and the bill is either sent to the floor or killed. On bills that are sent to the floor a document called a committee report is prepared, giving the committee's reasons for its actions. These reports are often obscure, not through any desire to confuse the issue but simply because the subject matter itself is obscure. Lawmaking is a tricky process, and even the lawmakers don't always fully grasp what is taking place within the committee rooms, as most of them will freely admit. "A lot of things go on in this subcommittee that I cannot understand," cried Representative Melvin Laird of Wisconsin piteously in the early 1960s, while on one of the House defense subcommittees. He then quit to become secretary of defense. This is not to put down Melvin Laird. It is simply proof that no one, not even the acknowledged congressional experts in a given field, really knows what is going on much of the time.

Up to the committee report stage, House and Senate procedures are strictly parallel; but now a variance occurs. In the Senate, the committee report and the bill will be sent directly to the floor to be scheduled for debate and a vote; in the House, the bill and its accompanying report make an extra stop in another committee. This committee, known as the Committee on Rules, has the task of determining how debate on the bill will be regulated once it reaches the floor. It does this by establishing a program, known as a rule, which tells how long debate will proceed on the bill, whether amendments will be in order and if so when and for how long, and when the final vote should be taken. This obviously gives the Rules Committee a considerable amount of power. If it doesn't like a bill, it can strait-jacket it with a rule so tight there is no room for its friends to maneuver it through on the floor. It can also refuse to grant a rule altogether, a procedure tantamount to killing the bill outright. (There is a procedure for bypassing the Rules Committee, but it requires a two-thirds favorable vote of the full House membership, something which is difficult to come by on issues which are even remotely controversial.)

Once the Rules Committee has cleared a bill for floor action, House and Senate procedures are again parallel; though there are major differences in the parliamentary rules for floor action in the two bodies, the actions themselves are nearly identical. Each may be thought of as a greatly expanded and tightly formalized committee markup session, with the committee consisting of the entire membership of the House or the Senate (the House even calls itself a "committee of the whole" for much of the debate). The bill is debated; amendments are offered, debated, and voted on; and finally the bill as a whole is voted on. If it fails, as in the earlier markup sessions, it is out; if it passes, it proceeds to the next stage, moving off the House and Senate floors and coming under the tender auspices of yet another committee.

This final committee is made necessary by the provisions of Article I, Section 7 of the Constitution, which speak of "a bill" which has passed the House and the Senate going to the president for his signature. What usually comes out of floor action in the two bodies is not *a* bill, but *two* bills, addressing the same subject in similar language but wildly disparate on specific points and sometimes even whole provisions. Some means must be provided to meld these two differing pieces of legislation into a single, unified bill, and it is from this constitutional need that the final committee, known as the House-Senate Conference Committee, has evolved. This committee differs in several important ways from all others in the legislative system. It is not a standing committee, but a throwback to the pre–Henry Clay days of a separate committee chosen for each bill. It holds no markup, has no power to kill a bill, and is strictly limited in its power to amend. If portions of the two bills it is trying to meld into one happen to be identical, it has no power to change or delete those portions. What power it does have, though, is close to infinite, in that its judgment and decisions are almost impossible to question. This power operates in those areas where the two bills passed by the House and Senate differ. In the gray area bounded by the House position on the one hand and the Senate position on the other, the Conference Committee has almost unlimited room to maneuver. Even when one house or the other has soundly rejected a concept in subcommittee, committee, and on the floor, it may yet find language establishing that concept forced down its throat if the other house has even tentatively embraced it. The Conference Committee is thus a sort of court of last resort for rejected amendments, and it should come as no surprise to find that membership on this committee is eagerly sought by sponsors of those amendments.

The product of the Conference Committee is the conference report, a document which contains the compromise bill adopted by the committee along with a synopsis of the reasoning behind the various compromises. This report is sent back to the two separate houses, where it is almost always considered under a process called suspension of the rules—no amendments, little or no debate, a two-thirds majority of both houses required for passage. One gets the impression that the members are getting profoundly tired of the whole thing by this time and want to get it out of the way as soon as possible. The conference report almost never fails to gather the necessary two-thirds majority very rapidly in both houses. When it has been cleared this one last time, it is finally ready for the president's signature and for incorporation into the United States Code of Statutes.

I suggested earlier that a productive means of looking at this maze of procedural steps and at the even larger maze of parliamentary rules which govern them would be to view it all as a sieve designed to catch and remove pork-barrel bills and other bad pieces of legislation before they are engraved in the law books. (This model should not be taken too far. Some of that extraordinarily complex machinery is there for other purposes, including that of expediting action on bills, which seems paradoxical until you realize that without the machinery the bills would not be likely to move at all.)

The great weight of the thirty-six steps that must be undertaken between a bill's conception and enactment, for instance, seems far more bearable when you realize that every one of those steps offers a new opportunity for the detection and eradication of pork-barrel provisions and other odious portions of the proposed law. Similarly, the fact that those thirty-six steps are contained within what is essentially two entirely separate filtration systems—one in the House and the other in the Senate—and that the bill must be independently forced through both, gives one a certain fail-safe feeling. The breakdown of one filtration system is not likely to lead to a breakdown in the other. The power of a senior senator to bull his way wholesale through the Senate filtration system, for instance, will mean next to nothing once the bill gets to the House. The reverse is also true, of course; no matter how much clout a member of the House of Representatives may have in his own body, when he steps over to the other side of the Capitol building he suddenly becomes little better than a tourist.

A closer look at some of the procedural steps and the history behind them also tends to bear out our analogy of a set of filters. And it supports our observation that Congress is well aware of the need for this filtration system and is actively working to improve it. Time and again, as you study the history of Congress over the first two hundred years of its existence, you can watch procedures and parliamentary rules either develop as a means of placing some control over the pork ethic or else, having been established for other reasons, be twisted to serve that role by later congressional leaders. A striking case in point is the evolution of power in the House Rules Committee, which was begun by a Speaker of the House who wished to use it to push pork through but which quickly became transformed by the House into an instrument to shunt pork aside instead.

As we have already seen, the birth of the Rules Committee came as a result of the first official action of the newly constituted House, an action the members viewed, quite rightly, as absolutely necessary if the House were to be able to function at all. From this auspicious beginning, however, the Rules Committee quickly degenerated in importance, and for the next hundred years it stumbled along as a sort of second-class power. It was still necessary—new rules were continually being suggested, and somebody had to be there to sort the wheat from the chaff—but it was far less desirable than those committees which dealt directly with issues and whose hands would be felt for years to come as they molded and shaped the law of the land. And that was how things stood until 1889, when Thomas B. Reed of Maine took the Speaker's chair and suddenly things around Rules got extraordinarily exciting.

Tom Reed was a Republican in a Republican era, but he was having trouble with the Democrats nevertheless. In those days, the great yawning gulf between the two parties came over the issue of tariffs: the Republicans were for them, the Democrats were against. Tariffs had begun in the early days of the republic as a means of raising revenue, but they had quickly evolved into a major pork-barrel issue. A tariff on glassware, for example, would discourage imports of foreign glass, thereby expanding the market for domestically produced glass. That was good for the glassmakers, and if you were a congressman with glassmakers in your district you knew what would happen to you if you didn't actively work to protect and increase those tariffs.

By Reed's time, the tariffs' revenue-raising function had been pretty well superceded. The Treasury had a big surplus, and the huge protective tariffs of the day—30 percent and more on many items—were simply pouring more money into that surplus year after year. A few years previously, beginning in 1884, the Democrats had enjoyed a brief fling at power under the presidency of Grover Cleveland, who advocated drastically lowering the tariffs and running the government on the surplus until it was used up. But Cleveland had been knocked out of office by Benjamin Harrison in 1888, and the Republicans were back in the saddle with every intention of riding the horse till she dropped. Far from lowering tariffs, Harrison wanted to push them still higher. The surplus? Parcel it out to the representatives and senators in the form of district projects —rivers and harbors work, roads, bridges, and so forth. It would be a pork barrel within a pork barrel, and things would be splendid for everyone, except for the poor citizens who would pay through the nose because of tariff-inflated prices.

As a good party man and a high-tariff supporter, Reed wanted to use his power as the newly elected Speaker to help push Harrison's tariff increases through. There was, however, a small problem: the House Democrats, who were resisting Reed's tariff bills with every parliamentary trick they could muster. Reed needed a way to push through that roadblock, and he found it in the much-neglected Rules Committee.

He began running every bill headed for the floor through the Rules Committee for a special rule which would shape the debate as he wanted it and either help pass it or fail it, depending upon which suited Reed's cause.

There were cries of pain from the congressional rank and file, of course, but they were of little consequence; Reed and the pork ethic were in command. "Gentlemen," he would announce calmly, as each new bill reached the floor, "we are about to perpetrate the following outrage," and then he would read the special rule that he and his friends on Rules had dreamed up. In this way the highest tariff rates of all time, the McKinley tariff (named after Reed's friend William McKinley of Ohio, the bill's sponsor in the House, later to become President McKinley and get shot) came into being. The voters showed their appreciation by putting Cleveland back in the White House and the Democrats back in control in 1892. But Reed's new use of the Rules Committee stayed. It was a good and necessary innovation—obstructionism on House votes had been getting rather out of hand. In addition, the antipork forces in Congress had discovered that, although Reed had instituted the new procedure to help him obtain pork, they could use it even more effectively to fight against it. This was done by packing the Rules Committee with gutsy representatives who weren't afraid to incur the wrath of their colleagues by refusing to grant a rule for a bill if it reeked too heavily of lard. The advantage of this to a congressman who wished to get credit for pork without adding too much to the federal budget was obvious. He could introduce a pork-barrel bill, push it through committee, watch the Rules Committee kill it, and take credit for his hard work for his constituents while the members of Rules took the flak.

The technique of the special rule, then—probably the

single biggest change in House procedure in the history of the body—can be seen as an example of a legislative step which began as a pork pump and ended as a pork filter. Similar courses can be traced for the development of many other congressional procedures. Suspension of the rules, for example—a technique by which bills may be brought to a vote on the floor without any parliamentary razzle-dazzle, just a straight up-or-down vote on suspension and then a straight up-or-down vote on the bill itself—was launched in 1822 by a desperate House which could no longer keep track of its own proliferating procedures and needed a way to go around them. But suspension rapidly became a pork filter par excellence through its strict prohibition of floor amendments, one of the chief ways a representative or senator who is not a member of the committee handling that particular bill has for tossing extra pork into the pot. The evolution of the congressional committee structure itself, from a special committee for each bill to standing committees and subcommittees, can be viewed in much the same way. Though its principal purpose is to keep the number of committees down to a manageable level (can you imagine a Congress with sixteen thousand committees?), it has also encouraged the development of specialists in certain types of legislation, an antipork move because a specialist is more likely to spot outrageously wasteful special-interest provisions in a bill than is a nonspecialist. The fixed committee structure has also prevented legislators with a porcine interest in a particular bill from forcing their way onto a special committee dealing with that bill in order to protect it on its way through—they are either on the committee to begin with, or they are not. But the best example of congressional procedure as pork filter is probably the development of the appropriations process in the two houses. Before we look at that development, though, we should take a close look at where that development has led: The appropriations process as it currently stands, together with the significant ways in which it differs from other, more run-of-the-mill congressional procedures.

The appropriations process, simply defined, is the federal government deciding how it is going to spend all that money you send it every April 15. It is a remarkably complex procedure, but it can be summarized fairly simply. The process begins deep within the bowels of the great federal agencies, a full year before the government sees your money and some eighteen months before any of it can be spent. Here in this bureaucratic inner sanctum the agency budget officers lurk, whole phalanxes of them for each agency, and here they go through the process of deciding how much money to ask for. This process boils down to (a) figuring out how much they would like to have, (b) figuring out how much they think they can get, and (c) submitting a figure someplace between the two.

The budget requests go to the Office of Management and Budget (OMB), the president's fiscal watchdog. The OMB pours them into a black box containing similar figures worked up by its own staff plus some general guidelines offered by the president and his advisors as to what the overall shape of federal spending should look like, and comes out with two budgets. One of these, the current services budget, consists of an aggregate of estimates as to how much it would cost to keep the government running at the same level it was when the budget was prepared, with no change in programs; it is shipped off to the House and Senate Budget Committees, where it quietly dies. The second budget contains the changes that the agencies and the president would like to see in current programs—increasing some, decreasing others, and adding new ones—and is submitted to Congress as the president's budget on or about January 15, roughly eight months after preparation began and ten months before the beginning of the fiscal year in which it will be used. This is sent down to the House and Senate Appropriations Committees, and the real fun begins.

A word should be said here about the great gulf which separates the Appropriations Committees from the so-called substantive committees—the committees which oversee the operations of the federal agencies, make the laws which regulate them, and have the power to set them up, alter them, or blast them out of existence. It is a gulf roughly comparable to that existing in theology between the elect and the damned. The difference is simple but profound. The Appropriations Committees have their hands on the public purse strings; the substantive committees do not.

Since nothing in government gets done without money, most of the substantive committees' power over their agencies depends on getting the Appropriations Committees to fund what they want funded and cut off funds for those programs they deem unworthy. The Appropriations Committees, on the other hand, while they cannot technically set up new programs, can increase an agency's budget over and above the substantive committees' requests in order to enable the agency to set up new programs on its own. Conversely, it can cut off funds to a particular program that the substantive committee may want very badly but the Appropriations Committee feels is unworthy. Hence the Appropriations Committees operate on a level far above the ordinary committee structure of the two houses. Four other committees operate up there part of the time: the two Budget Committees and the two committees (Ways and Means in the House, Finance in the Senate) which write tax legislation. But the Appropriations Committees are, for all practical purposes, the center of congressional power. When they get hold of the president's budget you can be quite sure that the president, the agencies, the substantive committees, and the Office of Management and the Budget are all well aware of that power and will do practically anything to make sure that the regal heads incline favorably in their direction. "Let's face it," one State Department official said of his Appropriations subcommittee chairman in 1958. "When Rooney whistles, we've just got to dance."

Anyway, once the president's budget is sent down to the Appropriations Committees, they hack it up into manageable chunks and parcel the pieces out to their various subcommittees, which begin holding hearings on them. The Senate is theoretically supposed to wait to begin work on appropriations measures until the House is done with them, because the Constitution specifies that all revenue-raising bills are to originate in the House. But this raises a number of practical problems, especially in regards to the logistics of out-of-town witnesses, and so the hearings are usually held concurrently. The Senate drafts no appropriations bills, however, but waits until the House has passed something and then uses that for its markup vehicle.

The subcommittee structures of the two Appropriations Committees are precisely parallel and are roughly parallel to the substantive committee makeup of both houses—there is one subcommittee in each house for appropriations concerning the Agriculture Department, another for the Defense Department, a third for Energy and Water Development, and so forth. The subcommittees listen to the witnesses, hold a markup session to draft legislation appropriating funds for the agencies under their jurisdiction (at levels which may or may not match the president's budget requests) and send them up to the full committee, which holds a markup of its own and ships the whole thing out to the floor. Here it will be considered, perhaps amended with a few extra pork-barrel items that several legislators think they are entitled to for their constituencies. (In the 1980 Omnibus Rivers and Harbors Appropriations Act, for example, four such amendments were offered and agreed to on the House floor, for two projects in California and one each in Illinois and Tennessee.) The bill is then sent to the president for his signature.

A close look at this complicated structure will show how tightly the pork filters interlock, and how many of them are built into the system. To begin with, there is the very important fact that the appropriations process is an entirely separate loop of procedures from the program-enactment mill presided over by the substantive committees. Recall our comparing that procedure to a two-stage fail-safe filtration system, with one set of filters in the House and another, entirely separate set in the Senate, both of which a program has to make it through before it can be enacted into law. If you compare the programs thus arrived at to filtrate trickling out the bottom of that system, and then imagine that filtrate poured back into the system for a second run-through—this time through the Appropriations Committee filters—you'll have a rough idea of the potential filtration efficiency of this separate appropriations process.

There are additional safeguards in the method the House uses for determining committee assignments for its members. These virtually guarantee that those who serve on the Appropriations Committee will serve on no other, thus insulating Appropriations Committee members from conflict-of-interest problems with other committees they might otherwise serve on. There is also the overview process provided by the Budget Committees, whose examination of the current services budget has at least the theoretical function of forcing Congress to take a look at where the aggregate total of bills that come out of the Appropriations Committees is taking the public purse. And since it should be obvious that a system this complex could not have developed overnight, but had to be sweated out bit by bit in response to particular needs, we might expect that a look at the history of those safeguards should give us considerable insight both into the safeguards themselves and into Congress's long-term response to the pork ethic. It does.

The story of the development of the appropriations process begins with the story of the development of the Constitution itself, and of the birth pangs that accompanied its formation. What Americans had obtained from the Treaty of Paris in 1783 was not really an independent nation but a conglomeration of thirteen semi-independent nation states ruled loosely and ineffectively by a weak Continental Congress under the agreement of association known as the Articles of Confederation. Those states spent most of the first six years of their joint independence from Great Britain jockeying for position within the framework of the Articles. It was pork at its worst—every state for itself and damn the expense to the others.

It only took a few years before the need for a strong central government became self-evident. When five of the thirteen states met in 1786 to draft a code of uniform trade regulations governing trade regulations amongst themselves and discovered that they were virtually unable to agree to anything because of pork-induced paralysis, self-evidence boiled over into action. The five states issued a call to the others for a constitutional convention. One year later, in May 1787, that convention was begun, with twelve of the thirteen states participating; the thirteenth, Rhode Island, declined to attend on the grounds that the convention was likely to cut into its rather lucrative foreign trade. Thus, before the convention had even started, the pork ethic was already cutting into its effectiveness.

Pork continued to be a major shaping force as the convention continued. The bigger states stubbornly refused to agree to anything that might reduce the advantage their size gave them over the smaller states. The smaller states just as stubbornly refused to let the bigger ones get away with anything that preserved that advantage. Inch by inch, clause by clause, over the four months the convention remained in session, a series of compromises was hammered out. The keystone of this series, known as the Connecticut Compromise (or the Great Compromise), was the development of a legislative system that essentially let both the big states and the little states get what they wanted. The big states got the House, where membership was apportioned by population and where their size would give them an advantage; the less populous states got the Senate, where membership was apportioned equally among the states. There they would coexist on equal footing with their larger neighbors. Thus the double filtration system we have described can be seen to have been built in by the conventioneers specifically to counteract the pork ethic.

Since a bill would have to pass both houses before it could become law, each group had a form of veto power over the other, and it didn't look as though anybody would be able to get away with anything; but just to make sure, a couple of additional safeguards were thrown in. Membership of the House would be determined by popular vote, but membership of the Senate would be determined by a vote of the state legislatures. (This latter idea proved a fiasco and was abandoned in favor of direct popular vote for senators on a statewide basis in 1913, but it seemed like a good idea at the time.) And "bills to raise revenue"—tax measures, tariff measures, and the like—were required to originate in the House. This was a sneaky trick by the big states to maintain control over the revenue-raising process; the House, after all, was supposed to be their bailiwick—but it backfired. Because the little states had had the foresight to insist that the House be elected by popular vote, the House early on came to recognize itself as representative of the people rather than the states. Members of the House knew better than to try to be extravagant with the people's money. Though later events, notably the popular election of senators and the development of a high proportion of "career" representatives (who depended on being reelected and who therefore had to pay more attention to pork for their districts) modified that image, its vestiges are still with us. Even today, the House tends to be more fiscally conservative than the Senate. In the 1979 National Taxpayers' Union voting study of Congress, which examined every spending vote of the 1978 session, House members averaged almost 18 percent more frugal than senators.

Although the makers of the Constitution went to great lengths to establish control over the power of taxation— they'd just come out of that war with England over taxation without representation, after all—they said very little about what should be done to spend that money once the taxation had raised it. They were content with a single clause (Article I, Section 9) stipulating that no funds could be released from the Treasury "but in Consequence of Appropriations made by Law."

The first few Congresses were nearly as lackadaisical. Laws would be made telling the executive branch what to do, and then almost as an afterthought a lump sum would be appropriated from the Treasury so that the executive could do it. Pork snuck in through the joints of this extremely loose process right from the beginning. One of the first acts of the new Congress, in 1789, was to provide the Maryland and Virginia delegations with a lighthouse at the mouth of Chesapeake Bay. But few people were paying much attention. One of those few, however, was a representative from Pennsylvania named Albert Gallatin, and after a few years of protesting and getting nowhere, he suddenly came into a position where he might be able to do something about it.

As a member of Congress, Gallatin had begun suggesting as early as 1796 that the lump-sum method of appropriations was a bit irresponsible, and that the secretary of the Treasury ought to be required to send down a set of itemized budget requests each year before Congress gave him anything to be treasurer of. No one, however, was buying it. Congress was still engaged in the delicate task of feeling out its relationship to the executive under the new Constitution and was in no mood to compel itemized requests. And when Gallatin took the idea up with President Adams's treasury secretary, Alexander Hamilton, he was practically laughed right out of the office. However, five years later Hamilton was laughing out of the other side of his mouth. Thomas Jefferson was elected president, and one of his early acts was to boot Hamilton out and replace him with Gallatin. The Pennsylvanian, of course, began at once to do what he had maintained that Hamilton should have been doing all along. Carefully itemized budget requests began coming down to Congress each year from the president. They have been coming ever since.

The immediate results of Gallatin's itemized budget were a mixed blessing, at least from the pork standpoint. Putting Congress on record as to where the money they voted to spend was going made them watch those spending votes a little more carefully—nobody likes to be caught voting for waste—but it also gave each congressman a new tool to impress his constituents. In that sense it might well be considered the foundation of modern pork barreling. Every district-specific federal expenditure forced onto that budget, then as now, was grist for the election mills back home.

But if the short-term effects were mixed, the long-term ones were far less so. Gallatin's innovation was the first step in the establishment of the single most important antipork weapon in congressional procedure: the insulation of the appropriations process from the authorizing process. From the itemized budget it was only a short step to itemized appropriations bills, and from itemized appropriations bills it was just one small step further to the formation of standing committees in each house of Congress to watchdog those itemizations. By 1816 this step had been taken with the formation of the Ways and Means Committee in the House and the Finance Committee in the Senate. Fifty years later the machinery was refined still further by the splitting of Ways and Means and Finance (both of which originally had jurisdiction over both revenue-raising and revenue-spending bills) to form separate Appropriations Committees in each house with the sole purpose of handling the spending function. All the machinery of the modern double-filtration system was essentially in place.

The propork forces fought back. Almost immediately there was grumbling that the newly formed Appropriations Committees were "too powerful," a phrase that can be translated to mean that they were blocking too many members' favorite projects. This grumbling reached crescendo levels by the 1880s. This was the era of the big tariff-induced surpluses, and most congressmen wanted those surpluses parceled out to them in the form of pork projects. The members of the Appropriations Committee weren't parceling. There was only one thing to do with a roadblock like that, and that was to get rid of it.

They did. In the mid 1880s the House moved to strip the Appropriations Committee of responsibility for virtually all substantive appropriations bills, shipping them out instead to seven substantive committees where they could be considered along with program authorization, thus short-circuiting the appropriations loop of the congressional filtration system. Sam Randall of Pennsylvania, chairman of the much-weakened Appropriations Committee, warned the members that they were being irresponsible, and that their action would inevitably lead to "extravagance." Randall was ignored, but he was right. Expenditures began climbing immediately; and ten years later, when the Senate Appropriations Committee was zapped in the same way by a floor charge led by one-term Idahonian Fred T. DuBois, they skyrocketed up still further. In 1880, total federal expenditures had been $268 million; by 1914, after twenty-five years of House experience with weakened pork filters and fifteen years of similar slapdashery in the Senate, yearly expenditures had almost tripled, to $735 million.

Then World War I came along, and the federal budget went through the roof—and didn't come back down. By 1921, federal spending was routinely topping $3 billion annually, and even die-hard porkers knew that something had to give. A chastened Congress passed the Budget and Accounting Act of 1921, formalizing Gallatin's century-old concept of the presidential budget and creating the Bureau of the Budget to oversee it. A year later, in 1922, the two Appropriations Committees stepped in with a sigh and took over responsibility for all appropriations bills again. They have held it ever since.

Minor readjustments have been made in the structure from time to time. The Legislative Reorganization Act of 1946 established the current parallel subcommittee structure in the two Appropriations Committees, and the Congressional Budget Act of 1976 created the House and Senate Budget Committees with budgetary overview function. But there have been no more raids on the rules by the propork forces. Since 1922, the filter mechanics of the appropriations process have remained essentially intact.

But this raises a question. If the appropriations process and the other congressional rules of procedure are such effective pork filters, and have been for the most part conscientiously designed that way, whence then the problem? If Congress has so carefully and deliberately been counterattacking the pork ethic for so many years, why does it remain so strong? Why is it that we still have so much pork-barrel legislation today?

The answer to that question should be embarrassing to Congress, but it probably isn't. The unhappy truth is that the formal rules and procedures of Congress do not really govern Congress. They are the rules within which the game is played, but they do not materially affect the outcome. Congressional rules are the public face of what is in reality an intensely private procedure: the crafting of legislation that will gain a congressman and his constituency the things they believe they want, while giving up a minimum of similar things to other congressmen and other constituencies.

In this game, as in any other, it is not rules that win, but strategies. These strategies have been developed and codified over time until they have come to encompass an entire body of unwritten rules and procedures which forms a complex infrastructure lurking just below the surface of congressional action. They guide that action far more thoroughly than do the written regulations by which the debates, committee markups, and votes proceed. And whereas the formal structure of Congress has taken on the aspects of a pork filter, the informal rules and regulations have far more of the attributes of a pump. They do not wrestle with the pork ethic, but embrace it, urge it forward, and in fact derive much of their strength from it. Occasionally they are practically synonymous with it. The story of pork barreling is the story of these informal procedures, and it cannot be understood apart from them. Logrolling, district inviolacy, reciprocity, chair supremacy, and all the others, large and small, make up the real procedural structure of Congress, and to these we must now turn.

4

Rendering the Lard

Sometime in the 1960s, while gathering material for a study of the Senate Appropriations Committee, Stephen Horn of the Brookings Institution had an interview with a man he later identified only as "a senior member of Appropriations' professional staff." Horn wanted to talk about subcommittee markup procedures, and his source was perfectly willing to do so, but he had a caveat he wanted to deliver along with his information. "Of course the real markup takes place prior to the meeting of the subcommittee," he told Horn, who subsequently reported the incident in his book *Unused Power.* "You're too late when you go into the subcommittee markup and ask for something. It's already been decided."

The meaning of that statement is clear. The formal decision-making apparatus of Congress, Horn's informant tells us, does not make decisions; it merely ratifies them. The real decisions are reached elsewhere. Where? Anyone who's been around Washington for very long can tell you. The decisions are made, for the most part, out of committee and off the floor, in small, informal meetings of senators and representatives and in staff strategy sessions. And they are made largely on the basis of an unwritten but highly structured and well-defined subset of congressional procedures which derives the greater part of its strength from the awesome power of the pork ethic.

The most important of these informal rules is the concept of district inviolacy, otherwise known as congressional courtesy or the reciprocity principle. Under any name, the rule is the same: What a congressman wants for his district or a senator wants for his state is not to be questioned by other congressmen and senators. If a representative wants a dam on a stream in his district, and if the Army Corps of Engineers or the Bureau of Reclamation can be induced to endorse it (not a difficult task), it will normally be built, regardless of need or of cheaper and better ways to accomplish the dam's purpose. Sometimes it will even be built if the Corps or the Bureau refuses to endorse it. If an airport needs repairs, or a harbor needs dredging, or a bridge needs building, a senator or representative can usually spring federal money free for that, too.

On the other hand, if there is something he thinks his district should *not* have, Congress will generally play along and not force him to accept it. This is especially true of restrictive land-use designations such as military reserves, parks, wilderness areas, wildlife refuges, and the like. Environmentalists seeking to establish wilderness areas in remote, unspoiled reaches of National Forest land have found it virtually impossible to do so without the support of the local congressional delegation. At the other end of the political spectrum, the navy's Project Sanguine, a land-based system for communicating with submarines at sea which would require large areas of relatively flat land for the creation of rectenna grids capable of receiving and sending powerful low-frequency radio waves, is currently resting in a sort of congressionally induced siting limbo. Several states' congressmen and senators decided they didn't want it messing up their landscape. The army is having similar difficulty locating congressional districts in which it can store chemical-warfare agents without having a law passed telling it to move the stuff elsewhere.

One fine June afternoon in 1979, while tourists filled the streets of Washington as the nation's capital basked through one of its rare periods of sparkling, smog-free weather, I sat in the House visitors' gallery and watched the district-inviolacy concept in operation. It was not a pretty sight. The occasion was the debate on Representative Bob Edgar's motion to delete funding for West Virginia's Stonewall Jackson Dam from the 1980 Energy and Water Resources Appropriations Bill, a motion whose overwhelming defeat I pointed to back in Chapter Two as an example of how deeply the pork ethic is engrained in the operations of Congress. The method used to enforce the ethic was a brazenly open appeal to the district-inviolacy principle. Edgar attempted to keep the debate centered on the merits of Stonewall Jackson itself, but it became evident about halfway through the debate that he was not going to be successful. The moment at which control was lost can be pinpointed with some accuracy; it coincided precisely with the entry into the argument of courtly, white-haired senior Congressman Harley O. Staggers of West Virginia, the representative in whose district the project is to be located.

Staggers's remarks were short, clear, to the point and entirely without reference to any facts about Stonewall Jackson except one: it was his. It was his, and Edgar had just darn well better keep his cotton-pickin' hands off. "When a congressman from another state tries to legislate what should or should not be in my district, I do not think that is right," the West Virginian said bluntly. "I certainly would not tell another congressman what to do in his district. . . . The governor of our state has endorsed this project. Our two senators have endorsed it. Our four congressmen have endorsed it. It is presumptuous to have someone from some other state tell us how to represent our state. I do not believe you would want somebody coming to your district from West Virginia and tell you how to represent it, not at all."

By using the word *senators,* Staggers had violated a long-standing House rule which insists that on the floor senators are only to be referred to delicately as "members of the other body," but that didn't matter. Edgar had violated a much larger one. Staggers had hardly stopped speaking when Don Young of Alaska was on his feet. "I know nothing of the project," Young said, "but what the gentleman just said in the well speaks very true of what I have been saying for the last eight years. It is time this body starts listening to the representative that represents that district. It is time we remember we are an elected body of representatives, not people who get involved and put their noses in something that is none of their darned business. That man over there was elected from that district. Let him speak for his people and if he says it is right, as far as I am concerned, it is right for the state of West Virginia!" It was all downhill from there. The dismal nature of the final vote spread has already been recorded.

The Staggers-Young pincers used on the Edgar amendment represent a blatant appeal to district inviolacy that is rather rare. (Though Young did come back the next day, in the wake of a similar, and similarly unsuccessful, attempt by Representative John J. Cavanaugh of Nebraska to delete funding for a project in the neighboring Nebraska constituency of Representative Virginia Smith, to offer what he called the "Pinocchio award" to be given monthly to the representative who stuck his nose the furthest into someone else's district.) The principle is always there, but it is usually well hidden behind several layers of disguise before a bill reaches the floor. Most of the district-inviolacy concept's work is not done directly, but through its influence on other informal congressional rules and techniques. Of these, the most important is undoubtedly the ancient, dishonorable and extremely widespread art of logrolling.

Logrolling, simply defined, is an unwritten compact in which two or more legislators agree to vote for each other's pet projects, thereby increasing the chances that both will pass. The technique and the term are both of great antiquity in American politics. One of the best early descriptions of the process dates from 1823, where it appeared on the front page of the Cincinnati *National Republic.* The metaphor, the paper said, was "borrowed from the customs of backwoodsmen. 'Do you help me roll my logs, and I'll help you roll yours.' This is the literal sense. 'Do you vote for my measure, and I'll vote for yours.' This is the metaphorical sense. This is legislative log-rolling; and in this manner are various acts . . . all rolled together in the statute books."

Clear as the *National Republic* was, though, it was not scoring a first with its description of the term. The usage of *logrolling* in its political sense dates from at least as early as 1809, when it was used in the title of a book called *The Legislative Log Roller,* by one Timothy Tickler, Esquire. And the practice of logrolling in the political sense is even older. In fact, though visitors to Washington, D.C. may not be aware of it as they stroll the wide tree-lined avenues and gape at the great marble buildings, they are walking through the results of one of the greatest logrolling compromise coups in the history of America: the 1790 vote of Congress which located the nation's capital on a piece of ground along the Potomac River so low and swampy that even today the western part of town, around the State Department and the Kennedy Center for the Performing Arts, goes by the unappetizing but apt title of Foggy Bottom.

The Great Federal District Fiasco had its roots in the trying period between the signing of the Declaration of Independence in 1776 and the ratification of the Constitution in 1788, while the country was under the somewhat uncertain rule of the Continental Congress. During those twelve years there was no permanent seat of federal government; the seat of government was wherever Congress happened to be meeting, which was never one place for very long. At various times, the honor of being the capital of the United States was claimed by eight separate cities: Philadelphia; New York City; Baltimore and Annapolis, Maryland; York and Lancaster, Pennsylvania; and Trenton and Princeton, New Jersey. This situation could not last and the legislators knew it. They had to settle down somewhere. The problem was that no one could agree upon just where.

The major problem the federal-city siters were facing was intersectional rivalry between the industrial North and the agrarian South. The seeds of the conflict that would nearly tear the country apart eighty years later had already been sown, and even then no one knew quite what to do with them. For a time it was seriously proposed that there be two capital cities, one in the North and the other in the South, with Congress apparently to be bounced back and forth between them like a gigantic political yoyo. A bill to set up this dual capital system actually passed the Continental Congress in the fall of 1783, and execution of it failed only because the numerically superior northerners made it quite clear that they intended their city, on the Delaware River near Trenton, New Jersey, to be the first among equals. That raised threats of secession from the southerners. The idea of a dual capital was dropped.

The issue stumbled along for the next several years, through the chaos of the Continental Congress years and the birth pangs of the constitutional convention. Then toward the close of the first session of the United States Congress in the summer of 1789, a bill passed which seemed to settle the federal city site once and for all; it directed that the capital be located on a plot of land near Germantown, Pennsylvania. For six months all seemed well. Congress adjourned, the members went off to their various homes and the people of Germantown began enthusiastically preparing for their role as the political center of the new nation. Then January 1790 rolled around, Congress reconvened, the southern bloc moved sucessfully to recommit the federal city bill, and all hell broke loose again.

Six months later, the battle was still raging. The southerners, who had coalesced behind a bill siting the capital somewhere "on the easterly bank of the Potomac," continued to lose close votes on passage but also continued to have the strength to block passage of any other siting bill. Finally, in late May, Thomas Jefferson, weary of the whole thing and fearful for the future of the infant republic, called a small dinner party at his apartment. The guests: Congressman Alexander Hamilton of New York and Congressmen Alexander White and Richard Bland Lee of Virginia. The day before, Hamilton had lost a close vote on an issue which he and Jefferson both considered vital to the nation's future, a bill calling for assumption of the Revolutionary War debts of the various states by the federal government. White and Lee had voted against the bill, but they were willing to change their votes—for a price. The price was Hamilton's delivery of enough northern votes to secure passage of the bill siting the capital on the Potomac.

Hamilton agreed, and by July he was able to deliver. The assumption bill went into the law books, and the Potomac became the site of the new federal capital. A few months later, George Washington went off to survey the area prior to making a final choice on the location of the city, and discovered that the "easterly bank of the Potomac" was mostly swampland. "I derived no great satisfaction from the review," he complained to his journal, but it was too late. The logs had been rolled, and that was where the cabin would be erected.

Modern logrolling does not differ significantly from the Hamilton-White-Lee deal that literally swamped the nation's capital in 1790. In fact, the principle remains identical: if you have a pet bill that you fear is several votes short of passage, look for those opponents whose opposition appears to be the weakest, find out what their pet projects are, and promise them your vote in return for theirs. And whereas the Federal District logrolling coalition might be excused on the grounds that the capital had to go somewhere, much modern logrolling does not even have this excuse. Examined on the basis of need, both bills in the Hamilton–Virginia delegation deal probably deserved to pass; examined on the same basis, bills in the majority of contemporary logrolling coalitions probably ought to fail.

A striking example of logrolling in which the taxpayer gets both ends of the log in his ear occurred in the Senate in the spring of 1979. At issue were four naval destroyers that the navy said it didn't want and an air force base that the air force said it ought to close. But when the logs had been rolled and the dust had settled, the navy had taken the destroyers, the air force still had the base, and the taxpayers had the job of providing both of them with what they didn't want with money the Treasury could ill afford to misallocate. There is no particular mystery about how it happened. The navy, air force, and taxpayers had simply come up against the combined forces of two of the most powerful men in the Senate, Budget Committee chairman Ed Muskie of Maine and Armed Services Committee chairman John Stennis of Mississippi. With that combination of forces, the match was hopeless from the beginning.

The story begins near the small town of Limestone, Maine, a mile and a half from the Canadian border and less than ten miles below the forty-seventh parallel. Here, in the cold-war hysteria following World War II, the air force established a Strategic Air Command base called Loring. At the time, it seemed like a good idea; but three decades later, with the waning of cold-war tensions, the changes in weaponry brought about by the development of intercontinental ballistic missiles and the fading of northern Europe as a political hot spot, the good idea had lost its luster. So the air force decided that it was time to close Loring down. Unfortunately, this would mean the withdrawal from northern Maine of a $46.2 million annual payroll spread over some 5,477 jobs. The Maine delegation, Ed Muskie included, promptly went up in smoke.

Meanwhile, several thousand miles to the south, a Mississippi shipyard was putting the finishing touches on four destroyers that had been ordered for the Iranian navy by Shah Mohammed Riza Pahlavi. All of a sudden the shah wasn't the shah any more. The shah was an exile, fleeing for his life to Mexico, and the new Iranian government had cancelled the destroyer order. Who would pay for the four almost completed ships? The shipyard appealed to Mississippi Senator John Stennis, who appealed to the navy, with mixed results. The navy might take two; it definitely did not want to be stuck with all four.

What happened next? I'll let Tom Dine of the Brookings Institution describe it. "Those four boats that had been ordered by Iran but then cancelled enabled Muskie and Stennis to make a deal in the Senate, whereby the First Concurrent Budget Resolution for Fiscal 1980, out of Mr. Muskie's committee, explicitly included funds for the navy to purchase those four boats. And in return, Mr. Stennis reported out a military construction bill which has a particular section in it which says, 'Loring Air Force Base shall not be closed.' Period. And screw you, air force." It was as simple as that. Muskie got his pork, Stennis got his. The logrolling worked like a charm, and only the taxpayers lost.

The Muskie-Stennis deal, you will note, was worked out on the committee level. Most logrolling is. And the reverse is also true: Most committee work is logrolling. A look-in on a committee markup session or on one of the negotiating marathons that go on in House-Senate conference committees can be an enlightening and sometimes sober-

ing experience. After sitting in on the conference to determine the First Concurrent Resolution on the Budget for
Fiscal 1980—the vehicle by which Ed Muskie saved Loring
—a UPI reporter wrote that it "resembled a horse-trading
session: shirt-sleeved committee members traded off billion-dollar programs and, for the sake of simplicity,
rounded off spending proposals to the nearest $100 mil-
lion."

Conference committee members' own view of their role
coincides closely with UPI's. "When you have different
things in dispute the two chairmen [of the House and Senate subcommittees] just trade them off, back and forth,"
one conference committee veteran told author Aaron Wildavsky. A similar view of subcommittee work was reported
to economist John Ferejohn: "There's the fellow who asked
me about a hospital he's got coming up," Ferejohn's informant explained. "Then when I want something done, I will
go and see him. . . . You traded back and forth across
subcommittees that way. It's a matter of scratching each
other's backs, I suppose. But that's the only way you get any
specific project accomplished around here."

Positive logrolling techniques like this will usually do the
job for a member who has a bill he wants to get passed. If
they fail, however, he can often fall back on the closely
related technique of negative logrolling: he can hold up
action on someone else's pet project until that person
agrees to vote for his. This works best, of course, if the
person invoking negative logrolling is in a position of
power—a committee chairman, or a member of the House
or Senate leadership.

A classic example of this occurred in the early 1960s
when Representative Mike Kirwan of Ohio, head of the
House Appropriations Committee's Subcommittee on
Public Works, chopped $1 million out of the water projects
budget for the state of Oregon in retaliation for Senator
Wayne Morse's negative vote on an aquarium Kirwan

wanted to see built in Washington, D.C. "I'll hold up all of Oregon's water projects until Wayne Morse learns something about fish," Kirwan snapped. Morse got the cuts restored without giving in to what he called Kirwan's "legislative blackmail," but he had to get the help of President Kennedy to do it. Others who came up against the Ohio tyrant were not so lucky. At the same time that Morse almost lost his Oregon water projects, Senator William Proxmire did lose a $3.8-million forest-products laboratory in Wisconsin. Like Morse, Proxmire had made the mistake of voting against Kirwan's aquarium. Kirwan's response was to remark, in conference, that if Mr. Proxmire wanted economy, Wisconsin seemed a good place to start. The forest-products laboratory went flying out the window.

A more recent example of reverse logrolling took place in the spring of 1979, when the Transportation Department decided that the AMTRAK service map should be trimmed to rid the agency of a number of routes which were plunging far into the red financially. One of the routes destined for the axe was the Mountaineer, a highly unprofitable run which just happened to go through Senate Majority Leader Robert Byrd's home state of West Virginia. It was slated for the axe—until Byrd got wind of it. "He let it be known," a Transportation official told me disgustedly a few months later, "that no transportation program in the country would run if the Mountaineer didn't. But that's the way things work around here. There are really only two legislative strategies in Washington: either everyone agrees, or something can be held hostage." Byrd's train is still running.

Besides being a splendid example of reverse logrolling, the Byrd/AMTRAK case illustrates another important principle of legislative deal-making: it is not necessary for both parties to the deal to be legislators. Along with assisting their colleagues in the House and Senate, congressmen can and often do roll logs with the executive branch of the government—the president and the great federal agencies. In this particular case the hostage threat was directed from Senator Byrd toward the Department of Transportation, but the reverse is also possible; the agencies are quite capable of holding congressmen's pet programs hostage in order to squeeze more money out of them. An oft-quoted example of this occurred in the spring of 1971 when Congress, trying to set up an austere Fiscal Year 1972 budget, threatened the National Park Service with deep funding cuts. The agency replied that if those cuts went through it would have no choice but to close the Washington Monument to tourists. Congress restored the funds.

The Byrd/AMTRAK case and the Park Service's Washington Monument gambit are both examples of reverse logrolling, but the positive form works just as well, and is found at least as often, between the legislative and executive branches. Presidents have been using logrolling to get their favorite programs through at least as far back as Abraham Lincoln, who used it to buy the three swing votes necessary to get Nevada admitted to the Union as a non-slave state, a step he felt was a crucial prelude to the Emancipation Proclamation. When Lincoln's envoy to the three wavering congressmen, Naval Secretary Charles A. Dana, asked him what they wanted, the president is said to have replied, "I don't know. It makes no difference. We must carry this vote or be compelled to raise another million men and fight, no one knows how long. It is a question of three votes or new armies. . . . Whatever promises you make I will perform."

More recently, Presidents Kennedy, Johnson, and Nixon were all accomplished practitioners of the art. Nixon, for example, once got on Air Force One with California Congressman Chet Holifield, who had been opposing Nixon's executive-branch reorganization scheme. The president boarded the plane as an opponent of further federal development of the breeder nuclear reactor; he got off committed to pushing the breeder program with all the power his administration could give it. Holifield, meanwhile, had mysteriously undergone a conversion, and now supported executive reorganization. It is hardly an accident that many of the breeder reactor parts would be manufactured by North American Rockwell, in Holifield's district.

Numerous stories are told of Kennedy's ability to deal presidential pork to congressmen in return for their favorable votes on his legislative program. There was, for example, a dam obtained by one southern congressman in return for a favorable vote on the president's aid-to-education program. As for Johnson, though the tales of presidentially hosted poker games in which the stakes were not money but public-works projects are certainly grossly exaggerated and probably apocryphal, it is known that he made a practice of punishing congressmen who refused to go along with him by going through the federal budget and personally slashing funds for projects in their districts.

But though many wasteful programs have certainly been logrolled into place by administration-congressional deals, it may be worth noting that they are sometimes better than the alternatives they supplant. Aaron Wildavsky tells the story of an unnamed Budget Bureau director who killed one of these logrolling schemes on the grounds that the two projects it authorized were extravagantly wasteful and served no good purpose. The agency protested that it didn't want the projects either, but that a pair of very powerful congressmen did, and that cutting them was actually likely to put more waste in the agency's budget rather than less. They were right. As soon as the budget got into committee the two powerful congressmen began logrolling with their colleagues in an effort to get the Budget Bureau's cuts restored, and when the dust had settled the two projects were back in place—along with seven others which had been used as bargaining chips to get the first two. The

Budget Bureau's cuts had parlayed two wasteful projects
into nine.

Next to logrolling, the most important technique for
forcing pork through the congressional filter is probably
that of the omnibus bill, also known as the "grab bag" or
the "Christmas tree." The theory behind these monstrosi-
ties is simple: if you pile enough pork onto a bill, nearly
every member of Congress will have something he wants in
it and cannot in good conscience vote against it, even if he
thinks some of the other projects it includes are absurd. It
is similar to logrolling in its reliance on gaining the support
of other congressmen by supporting something of theirs,
but it differs in one important way. By tying your project
and the project of the congressman from whom you want
support together into one bill, you have fixed it so that in
order to vote for his own project he *must* vote for yours.
There is thus no need to approach him directly for a conscious commitment which might mean reversing a previously stated stand or violating his ideological purity. The
omnibus bill is also more difficult to veto, both because it
tends to pass by a wide enough margin to make a veto
override by Congress almost certain, and because a president is likely to have a pet project or two of his own in there
which a veto would kill. All appropriations bills, and most
bills authorizing military or public-works construction projects, are of the omnibus variety.

The technique of crafting omnibus bills has not changed
significantly since 1868, when Representative Ransom H.
Gillette of New York described it in his book *Democracy in
the United States.* "Interest, and not principle, determines
what shall be done," Gillette wrote of the massive tariff bills
which were the common pork-barrel vehicles of his day. "If
votes from Louisiana and Texas are needed, sugar will
come in for favor. If support is needed from Illinois, Wisconsin, Minnesota, and Michigan, lead, copper, and pine

lumber are provided for. If the votes of Pennsylvania are
wanted, coal and iron receive full attention. . . . The principle of protection under a tariff never expands beyond the
objects necessary to carry the bill." Tariff bills are still put
together that way; "[multilateral trade negotiator Robert
S.] Strauss is obviously a master at understanding the pork-
barrel system," one public-interest lobbyist told me. But
today, the chief pork wagons—and hence, the omnibus
measures on which the most care is expended—are the
biennial Rivers and Harbors Authorization bill and its
closely related companion, the annual Energy and Water
Resources Appropriations bill.

The 1978 authorization bill was typical of the genre: it
included 68 projects, spread across all 50 states and affecting, in one way or another, nearly every one of the nation's
435 congressional districts. Many—perhaps most—of
these projects could not have withstood the scrutiny that
would have fallen on them had they been separated from
the omnibus bill and made to stand on their own. At least
three dozen of them had never been studied by the Corps
of Engineers, and hence no one, least of all Congress, had
more than the foggiest notion whether they could actually
be built. Nine of them were so economically marginal, even
by the loose standards normally used for these things, that
special formulas had to be written into the bill to allow
them to pass muster at all. (For several of them, the long-
standing law that benefits of water projects must exceed
their costs over the long run was simply waived.) One of the
projects called for the construction of a $45-million harbor
at Gulfport, Mississippi, $34 million of which would be for
the exclusive benefit of the E. I. Du Pont de Nemours
company; two others put on their pork-slab skates, hopped
on the hot skillet, and zipped right past federal cost-sharing
regulations to provide 100 percent free water to two communities in the district of ranking subcommittee Republican Bill Harsha of Ohio. The football huddle is said to have

been invented by members of a team in Georgia who, toward the end of a long and difficult game, had become so weary that they couldn't stand up without holding onto each other; this bill seems to have been put together in much the same way.

Bad as it was, though, the bill differed from others like it in only one major way: It failed to pass. The full story of that failure would take us too far afield; and I won't dwell on it here, except to point out that it was not due to any flaw in the concept of the omnibus bill, but to a series of judgmental errors on the part of the House and Senate leadership, the most important of which was timing. These public-works omnibus bills are traditionally brought up toward the end of the congressional session so that recalcitrant members can be kept in line with the threat of dropping their projects from the bill if they don't cooperate on other measures. In this case, though, the leadership called it too close. The bill came up toward the end of the last day of the session, enabling its small, dedicated band of congressional opponents to delay it to death through a series of parliamentary maneuvers which forced Congress to adjourn before the bill could be brought to a vote. Had the vote actually taken place, there is little doubt that it would have passed overwhelmingly—as usual.

A perusal of a pork-barrel omnibus bill or logrolling coalition always seems to turn up the fact that the members of the committee which deals with a given bill are particularly well provided for by that bill's contents. In Chapter Two, I discussed some of the patterns that have developed from this favoritism—how Department of Commerce spending averaged 40 percent higher in states with senators on the Senate Commerce Committee, how having a senator on the Military Construction Subcommittee of the Appropriations Committee was worth $1.3 billion to the average state, and so forth. I didn't cover water projects in that rundown, but it should come as no surprise that in this traditional pork-barrel area the principal of committee favoritism is extremely well established. Matching Corps of Engineers spending for 1976 with the makeup of the Senate Appropriations Committee's Subcommittee on Public Works reveals that:

- The fifteen states represented on the subcommittee, totaling 23 percent of the land area of the United States and 22 percent of its population, received 50 percent of the Corps of Engineers' spending for that year.
- The number-one and number-two members of the subcommittee, John Stennis of Mississippi and Warren Magnuson of Washington, represented the number-one and number-two states in Corps spending.
- Stennis, as chairman, pulled more than $186 million in Corps spending into his state; median spending, nationwide, was only about one-sixteenth of this, running between $11 and $12 million per state.
- The top five states in Corps spending—Mississippi, Washington, Missouri, Kentucky, and Louisiana—accounted for better than 46 percent of the total Corps budget. All but one of them were represented on the subcommittee; the odd man out, Missouri, was represented on the full Appropriations Committee.

Data on the House is harder to come by because federal spending figures are rarely broken down on a district-by-district basis, but the available information points in the same direction as that for the Senate. Much of that Mississippi spending, for example—including the $68-million 1976 construction budget for the $1.8-billion Tennessee-Tombigbee Waterway, the most expensive Corps project ever devised—was in the district of Representative Jamie Whitten, chairman of the House Appropriations Committee. A glance at a map of Ohio, which has twenty-three congressional districts, reveals that more than 70 percent of the Corps' spending in that state is concentrated in just one of them—District Six, in the south-central part of the state, which just happens to be the home district of Representative Bill Harsha, the House Public Works Committee's ranking Republican (yes, the same Bill Harsha whose idea of what his country could do for him included paying some of his constituents' water bills). An intense, in-depth study of water-project politics by political economist John A. Ferejohn, covering more than two decades' worth of records, concluded that membership on the House Public Works Committee "gains the member's state just under one . . . new [water project] start per year."

The reasons for this heavy committee favoritism lie in the way the sieve structure of Congress (which I explained in the last chapter) relates to the informal rules and mechanisms which make up the everyday working machinery of Congress. The committee is the chief component of this filtration system. Every bill must go through committee before it can get to the floor; the committee has the power to alter, block, or kill the bills under its jurisdiction. Most bills which die in Congress are killed in committee; conversely, most bills which clear committee will eventually pass. Committee members thus have enormous power over the issues which come before their committee, and, being human, they use that power selectively, to reward their friends, punish their enemies and, as one former Senate staff member put it, "to protect their political careers." (I hadn't quite caught the last word, and I asked him if he meant to say "rears" or "careers." He just laughed. "It's the same thing," he said.)

The committees, then, are not just a filter, but a *selective* filter, and much of Congress's attention is devoted to defining that selectivity and finding ways for non–committee members to get the bills they want passed out onto the floor in as intact form as possible. But all this attention, in turn, has served to focus the powers of the committees still further and thereby improved the committee members' ability to use those powers. It has become a positive-feedback loop, with the committees' powers feeding off the customs that have grown up to try to control them, until today those powers are nearly absolute in nature and often despotic in use. As I write this, a striking example of this despotism in action is underway in the Senate, where Oregon Senator Mark O. Hatfield has just pulled off one of the greatest pork-barrel coups of his long and productive career. Oregon is a logging and lumbering state; one-third of its economy is dependent, directly or indirectly, on the local forest products industry, which supplies the nation with fully one-fifth of its annual softwood sawtimber harvest. Federal laws which cater to that industry are among the major pork plums sought by the state's congressional delegation. Hatfield's most recent endeavor on its behalf, however, did not merely cater to the timber industry—it handed over most of the federal forest lands in the state to them, lock, stock, and pork barrel. In a striking throwback to the cut-and-run days of lumbering that everyone else thought had gone out with Gifford Pinchot (the pioneer forest-resources management expert of the early twentieth century), Hatfield's bill, under the guise of "wilderness" legislation, effectively prohibits the Forest Service from making any further land withdrawals for nonlogging use within the boundaries of the state of Oregon. Period. The senator has admitted to his colleagues on the Energy and Environment Committee that the bill has next to no public support and is opposed by all other members of the state's delegation, by the Forest Service (which would have to administer it) and even by portions of the timber industry. That opposition, though, doesn't matter: what matters is the senator's position as ranking minority member of the committee. Thus armed, Hatfield took advantage of an obscure loophole in the Senate rules known as the "clean bill" clause to move the bill *in committee* rather than through the

hopper on the floor. A few minutes later, the committee
reported it out—no hearings, no markup, not much of anything at all. Shortly thereafter, choosing a time when most
members of the Senate were engaged elsewhere, the
Oregonian took his bill up off the Senate calendar and,
after what Sierra Club lobbyist Doug Scott called "a profound and probing debate lasting precisely eight and one-
half minutes," rammed it through by voice vote. The whole
thing was over before opponents had time to do so much
as blink. The bill is now in the House, where alarmed conservationists are trying to bottle it up, without much hope
of success. Even if they do succeed, though, Hatfield has an
ace in the hole. "No Oregon wilderness bill," he has vowed
emphatically, "is going to pass without that clause in it
while I am in the Senate." Given the district-inviolacy principle and Hatfield's position on the committee that handles
wilderness bills, he is undoubtedly right.

The rules, formal and informal, that give a senator like
Mark Hatfield this kind of power cover nearly every aspect
of committee operation. Take the simple but extremely
important question of who should be on what committee,
or how Mr. Hatfield got to his position of power in the first
place. In the early days of Congress that task was handled
by the Speaker of the House and the President Pro Tem of
the Senate. This was fine as long as all committees were
select committees, invoked to handle a single bill and then
dissolved. But as the principle of standing committees
came to the fore in the early nineteenth century and the
standing committees evolved into bodies of specialists, the
fact that one man was making all the committee selections
in each house began to give him far too much power. By
the beginning of the twentieth century, things had pro-
gressed to the point where, as Representative George Hoar
of Massachusetts put it in 1907, "The career of a member
[of Congress] . . . is determined except in rare cases by his
assignment to committees." The presiding officers who did

the assigning were the objects of such fawning solicitude by those desiring choice committees that they had become virtual dictators.

Too much power was concentrated in one spot, and it couldn't last. A few years after Hoar wrote, the House rank and file revolted, pushing through a series of changes in the formal rules which set up many of the "pork filter" aspects of the modern committee system. One of those changes stripped the Speaker of his committee-assignment powers, giving those powers instead to the two major political parties through a pair of Committees on Committees composed of the leadership of each party caucus. The Senate followed suit a few years later.

Today, committee assignments continue to be made by each party's Committee on Committees, but there has grown up a complex web of formal rules and informal customs which strongly affect the committees' actions, virtually predetermining where a new member is to go as soon as he is elected. Most of this predetermination is based on the pork ethic, and it results in a member's getting on those committees which are most closely related to the business of his district, and through which he can do his district the most good. There is, for example, a well-established principle of states' rights to seats on certain committees. That's how Mark Hatfield got on the Energy and Environment Committee, which used to be the Interior Committee. This committee has traditionally been composed almost exclusively of Westerners. The Department of the Interior's principal divisions—the Bureau of Indian Affairs, the Bureau of Land Management, the Bureau of Reclamation, the National Park Service, the Bureau of Mines, and the Fish and Wildlife Service—are all far more active in the West than in the East. In a related technique, certain other committees give rights to a specified number of seats to proprietary interests which are regulated by the agency that they oversee. On the Agriculture Committee, for instance, membership rights go not to certain states but to certain crops or other agricultural products; there are corn seats, wheat seats, soybean seats, dairy seats, forestry seats, cotton seats and so forth.

In order to keep the barrel rolling smoothly through the committees, it is not only necessary that the committees include supporters of pork; it is also necessary that they exclude active opponents. To this end, there is often a tacit understanding between the Committee on Committees and certain powerful congressmen that these congressmen will have veto power over committee assignments in their area of interest. When John Watts of tobacco-growing Kentucky was chairman of the House Interstate and Foreign Commerce Committee, for example, it was understood that the Committee on Committees would not assign anyone to Watts's committee who didn't smoke and who might therefore choose to be harsh on the tobacco industry. Similarly, Sam Rayburn of oil-rich Texas was able, as Speaker of the House (and therefore automatically chairman of his party's Committee on Committees) to deny a seat on the House Ways and Means Committee to anyone who refused to support the oil-depletion allowance. In the Senate, Russell Long, who is not only from an oil-producing state (Louisiana) but is an oil millionaire himself, still manages as chairman of the Senate Finance Committee to exercise much the same sort of control over that committee's makeup. Rayburn made the oil-depletion allowance virtually attack-proof; Long has kept it that way. And that's the way it has gone for years, essentially throughout the entire Congress. "The Appropriations Committees and the authorizing committees," explains pork fighter Brent Blackwelder of the Environmental Policy Center in Washington, "are loaded with people of the pork-barrel mentality, and any potential critic of the program is kept off, screened off."

Because these rules are only informal—not officially codified or enforceable—they occasionally break down, al-

lowing a congressman to sneak through and get himself
assigned to a committee or subcommittee whose particular
variety of pork he wants to oppose rather than participate
in. When such mistakes happen, though, repair is usually
swift and inexorable. In 1974, for example, Representative
Bob Edgar, newly elected from Pennsylvania, managed to
win assignment to the House Public Works Committee's
Subcommittee on Water Resources. Most freshman members who found themselves in such an enviable position
would immediately begin raking in the pork for their districts in the form of those highly visible water projects.
Edgar did not. Instead, he used his subcommittee position
to attack the pork in other people's districts. This role, of
course, hardly endeared him to the committee leadership,
and they used their first opportunity—the subcommittee
assignment time at the beginning of the next Congress, in
1976—to strike back. "They shifted him right off the subcommittee," laments Blackwelder.

Sallie Phillips, Edgar's legislative aide for water resources, explains how the shift was accomplished. "Congressman Edgar had to list his three subcommittee preferences," she says. "He was unaware that if he had listed
Water Resources as his first or even second choice, he
would have been guaranteed that assignment because he
had served on it previously, and the subcommittee leadership did not advise him of the process. Instead, they used
the opportunity to move him off the subcommittee." Thus
are rules, maintained in letter, violated in spirit. "He didn't
even think it was an issue, remaining on the subcommittee," says Blackwelder sadly.

The committee leadership and the leadership of the
House and the Senate have the ability to control committee
membership along pork lines to a great extent, and even to
alter it in case the controls slip up. However, it is worth
noting that the same pork ethic which gives birth to the
controls in the first place also makes it so that they don't

have to be invoked very often. The scent of pork is such a powerful intoxicant that it is difficult for a congressman to resist being pulled into those committees where the aroma is most strongly directed toward his district. Like the sex-attractant scent given off by female moths, the smell of pork is so powerful that it can draw congressional moths of the proper species from three or four committees away.

"It is . . . naturally incumbent on a member to seek assignment to a committee which deals with legislation in which he has the greatest personal interest or experience, and preferably of a type that has some relevance to the problems of the district he represents," explains House Majority Leader Jim Wright in his book *You and Your Congressman.* Joel Aberbach, who studies committee structure and oversight at the Brookings Institution, agrees. "It's typical in Congress for people to seek committees that will benefit them in some way," Aberbach told me. "And so most of these committees in that sense are self-perpetuating, and they don't have to have a very vigorous enforcement mechanism to take care of the problem. Of course, there are people who join committees because of a policy interest, and that may run counter to the dominant policy interest. That does happen. But the typical person who wants to serve on the public-works committee is interested in seeing public works built. Or else he'd find it rather a drag. Given the nature of the committee, and the nature of most of the people who seek seats on a committee like that, it's a lonely life sitting there opposing what everybody else wants. And people grow tired of that, and they don't want to start it in the first place." Or as Senator Paul Douglas put it after six years of futile jabbing at the pork barrel, "You can't go on being Horatius at the bridge forever."

The reasons people with a pork interest in a certain policy field try so hard to get onto the committees dealing with that field, and why, once on, they work so hard to keep antipork people off, have to do, of course, with the great power those committees hold over the legislation before them. In the last chapter we discussed the basic necessity behind that power: the pork-filter need to reduce the flood of twenty thousand or so bills each year to the three or four hundred which will become law. Two additional points need to be made. The first is that, however avidly the members of a committee may ignore logrolling coalitions and the threat of retaliation from members of other committees to kill the bills of nonmembers, their own pet pork projects are not likely to be dropped. And the second is that, once the committee has decided to go with a bill, the same concentration of powers that can stop cold the bills the committee doesn't want to pass make those it *does* want to pass virtually unstoppable.

Take the role of the committee chairman. Necessity has turned this position into an extremely powerful legislative plug, making the person who occupies it capable of stopping virtually anything he doesn't like which falls within his committee's jurisdiction. Congressman Wright's book cites a splendid example of this power in action. House Judiciary Committee Chairman Emanuel Celler, when asked in 1958 about how he stood on a certain piece of legislation, replied, "I don't stand on it. I am sitting on it. It rests four-square under my fanny and will never see the light of day." It was probably under Celler that the Judiciary Committee began to be known among House wags as "the morgue" because it was the repository of so many dead bills.

A decade or so previously, Appropriations Committee Chairman John Taber of New York had used the power of his chairmanship to slash large chunks out of appropriations bills, earning the enmity of President Harry S. Truman (who referred to the process as "the Taber dance") and of so many others that a new word, *taberize,* was added to the House vocabulary. And there was Celler's contemporary, Rules Committee Chairman Howard Smith of Virginia, who developed the habit of being out of town when certain bills were due to be called up by his committee. The committee couldn't call itself into session without him, and the bill would die. "Just checking my hay crop," Smith would say guilelessly when he returned to Washington. Trouble was, of course, that his hay never seemed to need checking except when the bill due to come up before Rules was one he didn't like.

This bottle-stopper ability of the chairman means, of course, that many bills which might otherwise pass will fail. Curiously enough, though, it also has the reverse effect: Many bills which might otherwise fail will pass. The reason for this is simple. Because a committee chairman has that kind of power, none of the other 434 members of Congress or the other 99 senators wants to offend him, and consequently once a bill gets to the floor with his endorsement it is almost certain to pass by a rather large majority. If he is chairman of a particularly powerful committee like Appropriations, Finance, or Ways and Means, this rule can hold true even if the bill in question is running through someone else's committee.

I ran across an excellent example of this a few years ago while researching my book *Hells Canyon*, about the birth of the Hells Canyon National Recreation Area on the Idaho-Oregon border. The year was 1975, the National Recreation Area bill was going through committee, and its principal House sponsor, Representative Al Ullman of Oregon (the congressman from the Hells Canyon district) had just been made chairman of the House Ways and Means Committee. He was not a member of the Interior Committee, the panel handling the Hells Canyon legislation, but he had power there anyway, as the Pacific Northwest Power Company soon found out. The power company, whose plans for a pair of big privately constructed dams in the canyon would be thwarted if the bill went through intact, was attempting to amend it through a vehicle known as the Roncalio amendment so that one of the two dams would still be

constructable. This amendment failed by a very wide margin. Why? "I can give you a quotation which I think is the
best explanation of it," power-company attorney Hugh
Smith told me a few months later. "In the subcommittee in
the House we had a member from the Midwest who voted
for the Roncalio amendment, and in the full committee he
voted against it. He was asked after the full committee
adjourned, 'What happened?' and his answer was, 'The
chairman of the Ways and Means Committee tells me how
to vote on this bill.' " Ullman, Smith went on to explain,
had gotten himself into a public-relations bind whereby he
had to pass the bill intact, i.e., unamended, or suffer politically. The other members of the House knew this. They
also knew that, if they ever expected to get a revenue bill
past Ways and Means, they'd better play along on Hells
Canyon. When the National Recreation Area bill came up
for a vote of the full House, the margin of victory was
342–53.

The chairman is the most powerful member of the committee, but the other members aren't exactly powerless.
The ranking minority member—the member of the minority party with the greatest seniority on the committee—has
almost the same clout as the chairman. If the balance of
party power in Congress should change in the next election
he would become chairman, and everyone else wants to be
sure to remain on his good side in case this happens.

This reasoning extends downward several levels into the
ranks. Senator Hatfield is the number-two Republican on
the Senate Appropriations Committee, which is why a new
lighthouse was dedicated at Winchester, Oregon, in June
1979. In its report of that dedication, UPI quoted Senator
Bob Packwood, also of Oregon, who explained that Hatfield's position on the Appropriations Committee was the
key to getting the $16-million lighthouse built. "It makes
all the difference in the world," Packwood told the crowd
of assembled dignitaries. "That is why Mark is so critical to

this coast and this state." And that—take it from the pros like Packwood—is how you get bills passed in Washington.

Lower-ranking members of the committee aren't quite that deferentially treated, but they are not exactly powerless. One of the unofficial rules of procedure, for example, states that no floor amendment in either body of Congress will be seriously considered unless it is offered by a member of the committee the bill came out of. This prevents frivolous amendments from being offered willy-nilly by the rank and file membership, and this is good. But it also means that any non–committee member who wants to introduce a floor amendment must find a committee member to introduce it for him, and that is not so good. That means the committee member will have to be courted. The principal means of courtship is to offer a logrolling deal, and the principal purpose of virtually every logrolling deal is extra pork for those who roll the logs. So the frivolous amendments get in anyway—and they get passed. Most members of Congress rapidly become full-fledged masters at stroking the members of other committees. They have to, or lose all effectiveness for their own constituents.

Up to this point, we have been discussing the formal and informal rule structures of Congress as if they were separate systems. This is a valid model; they are separate, most of the time. But the line between them is very thin and often fuzzy, and there is one important congressional technique which sits squarely on top of that line and cannot be understood properly unless its line-sitting position is also understood. This bastard technique—neither fish nor fowl, formal nor informal—is the caucus.

If you reach for a dictionary and look up the word *caucus,* you may be misled. I have three dictionaries on my desk. They are of three different ages and come from three separate publishers, but they all define *caucus* in the same way: as (in the words of the 1977 *Funk & Wagnalls)* "a meeting of members of a political party to select candidates, plan a campaign, etc." That's a perfectly fine definition, but it doesn't cover the way the word is currently used in Washington. A caucus, in today's congressionalese, refers to the group of people doing the meeting, as well as to the meeting itself. The meeting, though it is always political, need not be limited to partisan issues. To put it in positive terms, the word *caucus* now means *a political group with more or less fixed membership which meets on a more or less regular basis cooperatively to promote matters of common concern.* In other words, a thinly disguised lobby, with the important difference that, whereas a lobby is composed of people trying to influence Congress, a caucus is composed of the congressmen themselves.

There are hundreds, perhaps thousands, of these caucuses in Congress. There is a House Democratic Caucus, a House Republican Caucus, a Senate Democratic Caucus and a Senate Republican Caucus, each composed of all members of the party's delegation and dedicated to promoting the official party platform. There are smaller splinter groups dedicated to promoting a particular viewpoint within the party, such as the Democrats' Democratic Study Group and the Republicans' Marching and Chowder Society. There is a Black caucus, an Italo-American caucus, a Polish-American caucus. There are caucuses devoted to broad policy issues such as foreign affairs, the environment and world peace. And prominent among them—in fact, probably numerically superior to all the rest put together—are the caucuses put together for pork purposes, whose binding strength is the pork ethic.

There are state caucuses, groups whose membership is composed of all members of a state's congressional delegation and whose purpose is to work together on "matters of mutual interest"—i.e., pork. There are also regional caucuses. The long-standing Southern Caucus is the best-known and most highly organized of these, but similar patterns of cooperation exist in other regions with overriding common problems such as the Southwest (aridity) and the Pacific Coast (fisheries and lumbering). There is an agricultural caucus, the Farm Bloc, which has recently tended to split up into smaller single-crop caucuses such as associations of wheat-producing states, corn-producing states and tobacco-producing states. Currently one of the hottest areas for caucus formation is the field of energy. "Energy policy on the Hill is divided up into feuding factions," a White House staff member told me in the summer of 1979. "They have a solar caucus, a gasohol caucus, a synfuels caucus, and so forth. Each of these areas has its own little fan club, and they're all vieing within Congress for money and support." In fact, the porkable area which does not have a caucus associated with it is exceedingly rare.

The strength of a caucus—its ability to shape legislation during markup sessions or influence votes in committee or on the floor—is based on the fact that its membership cuts across more than one formal congressional committee and level of seniority. Having a spread across several committees enables the caucus to have influence over legislation that comes before every one of those committees; having committee chairmen is even better. "I needed something from an agency," John Ferejohn quotes one New York Republican as saying. "One of our members is on the Appropriations subcommittee that handles that. I got him to help. They heard him fine while they seemed to have some trouble hearing me." The more committees your members are on, of course, the more legislation you can affect, and the larger caucuses often consciously attempt to get as wide a committee spread as possible. Seniority works in the same way. Members of the Oregon delegation, for instance, get better treatment on tax bills than most primarily because one of their members, Al Ullman, is chairman of the House Ways and Means Committee. And it certainly doesn't hurt the chances of any legislation affecting Massachusetts to have House Speaker Tip O'Neill as a member of its delegation.

In order to take advantage of committee membership spread and seniority clout, of course, a caucus must be rather cohesive. United we stand, divided we fall. Often this cohesiveness is enforced simply by common interest, but there are other means when that fails. Usually these boil down to a simple failure to cooperate. Logrolling coalitions magically dissolve, omnibus bills produced by the caucus somehow fail to include the recalcitrant member's project. The word gets around, and he has trouble joining other caucuses. Congressmen like Idaho's far-right "individualist Republican" Steve Symms are relatively powerless within the congressional body because, as one public-interest lobbyist put it to me, "He's simply too far out from the average crowd." He has violated the Rayburn maxim on going along if you want to get along a few times too many; he exercises what Speaker O'Neill once called his "daily routine of trying to prevent legislation from coming up" too often to expect anyone else to want to help him.

If the caucus in question is a state delegation, the member who strays may find it difficult to get reelected. In the machine days of New York politics, it is recorded that the delegation boss would occasionally harangue the assembled caucus with fist clenched: "Goddammit, you'll vote for this thing or you won't come back here!" Such days are not entirely dead. When Representative Bob Edgar took on the Stonewall Jackson Dam, for example, he found other members of the Pennsylvania delegation muttering dire things about him. "Members from Pittsburgh," explains Brent Blackwelder, "claimed that somehow retrofitting an aircraft carrier in Philadelphia was being aided by the guy in West Virginia whose project was being attacked, and Edgar was breaking up this big logrolling coalition that had been established, and it was a disaster, and if Edgar hoped to run for the Senate he'd better not start making any enemies around the state." It was no accident that when Edgar persisted—"Congressman Edgar doesn't go for the district-alone concept," explains Sallie Phillips, because "all taxpayers must pay for these projects, and therefore every congressman has a responsibility to his own constituents to see that this money is spent wisely"—two of the congressmen who attacked him the most strongly on the floor were fellow Pennsylvanians.

I have mentioned that the technique of the caucus is a sort of cross-breed between the formal and informal rule structures of Congress which partakes of the power of both. Most caucuses are quite tightly organized, with officers, bylaws, and all the accouterments of official societies; the larger ones even have their own whip systems to alert caucus members to legislation of mutual interest that is coming up for floor action. This tends to give them a quasi-official standing within Congress and to allow them to act as a part of the formal power structure. On the other hand, most of their clout is derived from the strengths that their cohesiveness gives them within the informal power structure: building logrolling coalitions, shaping omnibus bills, blocking legislation which seems inimical to them or which can be held hostage for something they want from another caucus. And clout is what they wanted when they formed the caucus in the first place. There is a quotation that illustrates this nicely. It comes from a Public Works Committee chairman who was asked why he allowed his committee to endorse so many wasteful water projects in so many parts of the country. Why, the questioner asked, did other congressmen get so much out of him? His reply was candid: "It's easier to give it to them than to keep it from them," he said. "So we give it to them."

Congressmen form caucuses, roll logs, craft omnibus bills, and manipulate all the other creative power tricks this chapter has discussed largely to get into a position where it is easier to give things to them than to keep them away.

When it becomes easier to give than to withhold, more things are given. The pork barrel and the federal budget may both bulge ominously, but this doesn't seem to matter. As long as each congressman gets the federal plums his district or state wants, his function as a representative of his constituents is being fulfilled.

But this raises another major question. A congressman fulfils his duties as a representative of his district or state by giving his constituents what they want out of the federal grab bag. Very well. But how does he determine what they want? How does he decide whether the people he represents would rather have a dam or a free-flowing river, a bridge or a forest-research laboratory, a Tennessee-Tombigbee Waterway or a $1.8-billion reduction in the federal budget? Who does he listen to? When the pork ethic whistles, what forces within his district tell him which way to dance?

We've talked about why the pork ethic is so powerful and how a congressman functions within the congressional structure to make sure he gets his share of the pork. Now it is time to discuss the even more difficult question of who gets the pork after it is delivered, and who determines what to order in the first place. The answers are not as black and white as they are generally made to appear.

5
A Triangle of Iron

In 1974, I was one of a delegation of southern Oregon environmentalists who paid a call on the Democratic candidate for Congress from our district, a Eugene builder named Jim Weaver. What, we wanted to know, was he going to do for us if he managed to get elected? His answer was candid. "I'd like to do just about all I can for you," he said. "I agree with you on most of the issues, and I need your support. But, you know, I need organized labor, too, and I want to do what I can for them. And every time I approach you guys, someone from labor is sure to come up to me at some cocktail party and say, 'Weaver, you're in bed with the birdwatchers again.'"

Weaver went on to win that election, and every election since, presumably with the help of both organized labor and the birdwatchers. But that is not the point. The point is that even as a candidate—not yet a congressman—Weaver was getting conflicting views concerning what was best for the district, from district residents whose integrity he respected, whose support he wanted, and whose views on the issues he couldn't get to agree to save his soul. And

101

if it's like that for a mere candidate, imagine what it must be like once the candidate wins his election and becomes a congressman.

The average congressional district is made up of approximately 535,000 diverse opinions on every conceivable issue. Some of the people in the district are farmers who will be sure that a big federal dam is just what they need to control flooding in their fields; others are fishermen who are equally sure that the same dam will ruin the river. Some are people who sell things, and who are keeping a sharp eye on the laws regulating retail trade; others are people who buy things, and they'll be keeping an eye on the same laws but for different reasons. Some residents of the district will welcome a nuclear submarine base with open arms, as a demonstration of American might and as a boost to the local economy; others will see it as a threat to world peace and won't want the thing there or anywhere else if they can help it. The urban residents will welcome federal aid to mass transit; the rural residents would rather see the same money spent on highways. Caught in the middle of these conflicting demands, the congressman has a real problem. The pork ethic demands that he do something for the district. What should that something be? Whom should he listen to to find out?

Well, if he's human—and congressmen are—he's going to answer that last question in one of two ways. He's either going to listen to (a) those who shout the loudest or (b) those whose judgment he trusts the most, which usually means those whose opinions agree with his own ("You must be right—your arguments make such good sense"). The trouble is that neither of these groups necessarily holds a majority in the district. Even if they do, there is no guarantee that what they want is what the district actually needs. Constituents ask for some strange and often conflicting things, and no law says that what they ask for has to make sense. "The polls show that people want their government reduced, but they also want their government to do more for them," says Common Cause lobbyist Jane Wishner in Washington. "And that's a basic fundamental inconsistency which is perfectly understandable, but which must drive political figures absolutely crazy. Listening to some of the members of Congress talk about the balanced budget, we hear things like, 'My God, I have constituents write to me all the time, saying, You've got to balance the federal budget and cut down federal spending, and by the way, our local hospital needs some work . . .' But that's the dilemma they face, and that's what makes discipline so tough." All of which puts us right back to square one. We still don't know what the constituents want. In fact, they don't even know what they want themselves. What next?

It is at about this point that most congressmen give up, loose their grip on their ideals, and allow themselves to be pulled gracefully downwards into the grip of the pork-barrel mechanism that pork fighters fear most—a tight three-way configuration of lobbyists, congressmen, and federal-agency personnel known unaffectionately as the Iron Triangle.

It was George Pring who first introduced me to the Triangle. Pring is a tall, sandy-haired attorney with a mordant wit and a penchant for muted plaid sport jackets who operates out of a casual office a few blocks from the Colorado state capitol in Denver. The plaque on the door reads Environmental Defense Fund. The Fund is a national organization which specializes in environmental litigation, and Pring is their man in Denver for water projects, a position which has made him, not surprisingly, one of the nation's foremost experts on the pork barrel. "The Iron Triangle," he told me, leaning back in the swivel chair in front of his cluttered roll-top desk, "is a three-cornered political science diagram, if you will, with the congressperson whose district you're in at the apex. In the lower right-hand corner

are the beneficiaries—the local users' group, the lobbyists
—and in the lower left-hand corner is the federal agency
which will build the project, which in our case is usually the
Bureau of Reclamation. . . . the lines of mutual support *work*
just like a triangle." He grinned. "Unfortunately, engineers
tell me that a triangle is the strongest and least destructible
unit of construction."

In engineering, a triangle derives its strength from the
fact that each point is bound to the other two by a set of
rigid objects which assures that a force applied to any one
point will be felt equally by all three. The Iron Triangle
works much the same way, except that the binding material
is not a set of rigid objects but a mutually felt need for the
pork-barrel project. Each member of the triumvirate feels
this need for his own reasons. "The congressman needs it,"
says Pring, "because he needs the votes of the local constituency—as well as a little less-tangible factor, the need to
appear effective, even to constituents outside the benefit
area. You know, 'Old Joe can get it when we need it. Now
he just took care of those boys, and if *we* need it let's get
him reelected, because we don't want some young wet-
behind-the-ears kid in there who'll be tripping over his own
feet for ten years before he gets on the right committee.'
The local users' group needs it because they need that
tremendous infusion of federal subsidy, and the agency
needs it because—well, because the agency really only has
two choices. It either has to find a constituency to build new
projects for, or go out of business. The latter, of course,
being a fate worse than death in Washington."

Enclosed in this matrix of self-interest, each one perceiv-
ing that the only way to get what is wanted is to look for
support from the other two, the congressman, the beneficiary groups, and the agency form a tight little structure
which cannot be attacked at any one point without involving the other two. Accuse the agency of manipulating
figures in order to prove the "need" for the pork barrel,

and both the congressman and the lobbyists will immediately release flowery statements praising the agency's professionalism and sense of duty. Accuse the lobbyists of sticking their hands in the public pocket for their own private benefit, and both agency and congressman will counter with accolades to the lobbyists' public-spirited sacrifice for putting in all those hours and hours of work on behalf of this great public-works project. Accuse the congressman of playing politics—of pushing pork just to get himself reelected—and the lobbyists and the agency will fall all over themselves to remind the world of the congressman's statesmanship and effectiveness, the latter being measured, of course, by how much federal money he has managed to bring into the district and therefore, under the circumstances, being extremely difficult to argue with.

Projects can and do originate in any corner of the Iron Triangle. Sometimes a congressman himself will spot a legislative gambit which will increase the federal funds flowing into his district and therefore make him appear more effective. Sometimes a group of his constituents will approach the congressman with an idea, and sometimes the idea will originate in the agency's planning department, which, cynics maintain, often seems more dedicated to planning for the agency's survival than for the nation's benefit. Of these three possible points of origin, however, the most commonly occurring—the one responsible for a greater amount of pork, by several orders of magnitude, than the other two put together—is the constituent group. Therefore the logical spot to begin an examination of the mechanics of the Iron Triangle is with this group: a hodgepodge of direct project beneficiaries, local boomers, potential labor and material suppliers, and national trade organizations known collectively as the pork lobby.

The term *lobbyist* has been a dirty word in the American political lexicon almost since the birth of the republic. As

early as 1822, Senator Thomas Hart Benton of Missouri, a
granduncle of the twentieth-century American painter of
the same name, observed that "those interested" in a certain Indians' rights bill were "vigilant and active" in the
halls of Congress. Benton didn't use the word *lobby*, but his
contemporary, Senator Rufus King of New York, did, writing the same year of "Lobby agents and speculators" who
were backing a banking bill. By 1823 they were being referred to in the nation's press as "lobby-members," a term
whose genesis was explained a few years later by James
Kirke Paulding, a naval officer and novelist who later became secretary of the navy under President Martin Van
Buren. "They are called by way of honorable distinction
Lobby-members," wrote Paulding, "because they form a
sort of third estate, or legislative chamber in the lobby."

Sometime in the next few decades, *lobby-member* was replaced by the modern *lobbyist.* Author Neil MacNeill claims
evidence for its use as early as 1832, and it was certainly in
common currency by 1869, when Massachusetts Representative George Hoar complained that "the corridors of
the Capitol and the committee rooms were crowded with
lobbyists" and the New York *Tribune* referred scathingly to
"that higher legislative body the Lobby."

Early lobbyists' techniques were often coarse, running
heavily to such gambits as cash bribes, florid dinner parties,
and the procurement of willing women, and they and the
politicians they purchased were usually strongly looked
down upon by honest citizens. This activity reached a ze-
nith toward the end of the nineteenth century in the Senate,
which by the last two decades of that century was openly in
the hands of special interests. Senators were elected (more
accurately, appointed) by state legislatures. What the framers of the Constitution had in mind when they set up this
provision was a voice for each state government in the
federal legislature. What they got, in an era of expansion-
ism, cartels, and laissez faire politics, was a voice for the

principal industry of each state in the federal legislature. Ohio sent oilmen; Nevada sent silver-mine owners; Maine, Michigan, and Oregon sent lumber barons; New York sent bankers. It was in a very real sense the ultimate pork barrel, a legislature of lobbyists, and it could not last.

As early as 1828, a constitutional amendment had been proposed to change the electorate of senators to the state's population rather than to its legislature. In the nine years between 1893 and 1902, amendments to that effect passed the House of Representatives no less than five times, only to die an ignoble death in the Senate, where the special interests were not about to give up their power. Thwarted there, supporters of the amendment turned to the states themselves, seeking support of enough state legislatures to call a constitutional convention. By 1911 a convention had gathered enough steam behind it to worry the Senate. That spring, the crowning blow came with the publication of a series of articles in the Chicago *Tribune* proving that the 1910 Illinois senatorial election had been purchased outright by wholesale bribery of the state legislature. Senate resistance to housecleaning collapsed, and the direct-election amendment whipped through both houses and was sent out to the states.

Ratification came rapidly, and by May 1913, the amendment was part of the Constitution. With it came a whole new relationship between the legislative process and the lobbies. Though humorists would continue for generations to refer to Congress, with Will Rogers, as "the best that money can buy," the era of outright vote purchase—with the exception of a few notable lapses such as Koreagate and the Talmadge scandals—was over.

Lobbyists, however, remained as busy as ever.

Brent Blackwelder is a tall, slender, dedicated man with a thick shock of black hair and an advanced degree in mathematics who has been chief water pork-barrel fighter for the

Environmental Policy Center for the past ten years. His position has brought him into frequent contact with the special-interest lobbyists. Asked to describe what he has seen, he waves his hands expansively. "The special interests," he says, "are wide-ranging. We've found them from a paper company or a landowner to big banks, big construction firms, or whatever. Some real-estate speculator, maybe, selling lots around the lake." He ticks off specific examples: U. S. Steel's pushing winter navigation improvements on the St. Lawrence Seaway; E. I. Du Pont's seeking harbor improvements for its new plant in Gulfport, Mississippi; Westvaco Paper Company's supporting Gathright Dam in Virginia as a means of flushing their manufacturing wastes downstream into the Atlantic Ocean; "two oil rig manufacturing companies who want a quicker route to the Gulf of Mexico" planning the destruction of three bayous in Louisiana which together form one of the greatest natural wetlands remaining in the Southeast. All these projects, of course, would be accomplished by federal agencies using federal funds for the primary benefit of a few monied private interests. Blackwelder is convinced that this pattern holds true for nearly all federal water projects. "Scratch the surface," he says, "and there's some special interests who stand to make a mint. And that's what's kept it going over the years."

Water projects aren't the only type of pork that gets pushed by monied special interests for their own benefit. All across the political spectrum, behind nearly every bill that either deals with the distribution of federal funds or the regulation of private ones, the special interests line up. Aerospace firms such as Boeing and Lockheed lobby for military contracts, sugar-beet growers lobby for price supports and protective tariffs, automobile manufacturers lobby for relaxed clean-air standards, road builders lobby for the Highway Trust Fund. In most such cases, the resulting legislation clearly qualifies as pork barrel, with the prime beneficiaries clustered in a few states whose congressional delegations are the principal sponsors of the legislation. Nearly one-third of the working force in New Hampshire, for example, is employed in the shoe industry; under these circumstances, it is hardly surprising to find the New Hampshire delegation fighting hard for laws protecting the shoe trade. ("The position of the shoe industry," blustered one of them not long ago, "is a matter of urgent concern to many American communities." Especially those which are home to New Hampshire's fifty-five shoe-manufacturing plants.)

Similar forces are clearly at work when the Wisconsin delegation fights for price supports on dairy products, or when the West Virginia delegation seeks to weaken laws regulating coal mining and use, or when the delegation from Nevada, where 87 percent of the land is federally owned and four-fifths of the agricultural income derives from beef cattle, adamantly opposes laws proposing to charge ranchers fair-market fees for the use of public grazing allotments. It was legislative histories such as these that Common Cause president David R. Cohen had in mind when he warned, in remarks prepared for testimony before the House Budget Committee in June 1979, of "the power of special-interest groups to influence government decisions in which they have a major economic stake," a power which he stated had turned Congress into a "special-interest state." The extent of this special-interest state was demonstrated in a 1972 survey by Ralph Nader's Congress Project (now Congress Watch) which found more than five thousand lobbyists prowling the halls of Washington, including representatives of at least eight hundred of the thousand richest corporations in America.

But concentrating on those with a specific economic axe to grind doesn't tell the whole story of the pork-barrel lobby and its influence on the American legislative process. There is another side to pork-barrel lobbying that accounts for a high proportion of those forty-two hundred other registered lobbyists turned up by the Nader survey. This side is composed of individuals and organizations with a *generalized* economic axe to grind, a group known collectively to economists and others as *secondary beneficiaries.*

"You've got to remember," says Don Dillon, playing with a pencil on the big desk in his windowless Pentagon office, "that any public-works project which produces national benefits is going to produce those benefits through increasing productivity and revenues in some local area." Dillon holds a position with the somewhat unwieldy title of Deputy for Policy, Planning, and Legislative Affairs, Office of the Assistant Secretary of the Army for Public Works. In practice, this means that he is the army's civil-works lobbyist. Civil works, to the army, means principally the Corps of Engineers, and though Dillon takes pains to point out that he is not a member of the Corps, he freely admits his close relationship with them ("If it weren't for the Corps, I wouldn't have a job"). The Corps' project-justification procedures often depend heavily on secondary beneficiaries, and Dillon has become an expert in explaining them. He does so eagerly.

"Take navigation projects," he says about two minutes after we have been introduced and have settled down with the tape recorder between us. "Our criteria for a valid federal interest in a navigation project is that it has to have more than one user. So the policy would be that we would recommend and propose dredging a channel that has two or more industries projected to use it. So in that case, as far as primary beneficiaries are concerned, you would have two or three or four or five, or half a dozen, or such as that. But the goods that they carry—if they are carried more efficiently by the waterway than by some alternative form of transportation, truck or rail or whatever—the savings in transportation costs would be counted as a national benefit, a benefit to the nation. Presumably their goods would be produced less expensively, and the costs of producing the goods would be deflected downward—so the cost to the nation would be reflected in the transportation rates."

In Dillon's example, the primary beneficiaries are the barge companies who use the canal; the secondary beneficiaries are the consumers whose goods are presumably cheaper because they are carried on barges rather than on railroads or trucks. That's one form of secondary beneficiary, but there are many others. In Denver, from a standpoint that is essentially diametrically opposed to Dillon's, George Pring points out a few. "They are," he says, "the local chamber of commerce, the local head of your general store, the local filling-station gas jockey—many of them very solid citizens, pillars of the community, good fathers, don't beat their wives, nice folks—who see that somehow the community stands to benefit from this public-works project in a fashion that will indirectly benefit them economically. Maybe it'll put them back on the map, in the case of a road; maybe it'll pull in new businesses. Maybe they just forsee an opportunity to make a big killing while the construction crews are in town." They are, in other words, everyone whose business stands to gain not from the project itself, but from the extra business the project is expected to draw into the area. They look for what they call an "improvement in the economic climate." They hope that this meteorological improvement means that it is going to rain money, and just in case, they're going to rush out there to the downspout with a big bucket.

Many groups lobby for secondary beneficiaries in Washington. Many do little else. There is, for example, the National Chamber of Commerce, a fixture in Washington since the 1930s in its huge neo-Corinthian mausoleum across Lafayette Square from the White House. There is the National Alliance of Businessmen, the National Association of Businessmen, the National Independent Businessmen's Association. There are local-government lobbies such as the National Association of State Development Agencies, the National League of Cities, the National Association of Towns and Township Officials, and the National Governors' Association. There are lobbies for industries which relate to government spending primarily on a secondary-beneficiary level, groups like the National Association for Uniformed Services, the National American Wholesale Grocers' Association, the National Association of Credit Union Supervisors, and the National Association of Truck Stop Operators.

There are lobbies for groups which act as primary beneficiaries under certain pieces of legislation and secondary beneficiaries under others: oil companies (primary—the oil depletion allowance, secondary—the highway trust fund), coal companies (primary—strip mine laws, secondary—federal barge canals in coal country), construction workers' unions (primary—*common situs* picketing, secondary—public-works projects involving structures of any size), and a whole host of others. There are, in fact, twenty-five columns of "National This" and "National That" in the District of Columbia phone directory—nearly every one a lobby, nearly every one, at one time or another, a secondary beneficiary. All of these can be validly counted as part of the pork lobby. There is little wonder that the pressure on Congress is so intense.

At this point, however, a word of caution. We have established that the lobbying presence in Washington is huge, that the roots of lobbying go very deep into American political history, and that lobbyists represent an almost bewildering variety of special interests. From these facts, and from the pejorative overtones that the word *lobbyist* usually seems to have both in daily usage and in political novels, it would be easy to leap to the conclusion that the average lobbyist is a nasty sort of fellow oozing around the halls of Congress like a seller of French postcards, twirling his moustache with unsavory glee as he plots nefarious ways to rip off the American taxpayer to obtain windfall profits for the people who have hired him. But this picture, common as it is, is largely false; though there are a few lobbyists who see themselves in this role, most would be appalled by it.

The typical lobbyist, especially if he is representing a secondary beneficiary, is convinced that the course he advocates is beneficial to the nation as a whole and is therefore a legitimate use of public funds. "They weigh the benefits differently," says Joel Aberbach of the Brookings Institution. "They don't look at it the way you might look at it, or the way I might look at it. It's self-serving, obviously —but many of them have convinced themselves that the building of physical structures is a real benefit, and they consider it a very legitimate function. So they're not necessarily pushing for something that is a great benefit to a small number of people, and greatly opposed by a large group of people." Instead, they are pushing for something which they sincerely believe to be in the best interests of society. The problem is that the various lobbyists view those best interests through sets of selective lenses created by their special-interest associations. "Don't forget," the army's Don Dillon reminds us, "environmentalists are lobbyists, too."

But if this is true, whence then the problem? If all lobbyists are equally convinced that the course they advocate is best for the nation, and if environmentalists and other public-interest groups are lobbyists, too, why is it the pork lobby that has worked its way into that lower right-hand corner of the Iron Triangle instead of one of the others? And for that matter, who says they shouldn't be there? If each individual pork lobbyist is such a nice, sincere guy, why is the pork lobby as a whole so pernicious?

That question can be answered with one word. The word is *concentration*. The pork lobby has it. The public-interest lobby does not.

Deep down in the ghetto on the "wrong end" of Pennsylvania Avenue in Washington, in a pair of side-by-side converted townhouses that serve as the head office for the National Taxpayers' Union, I paid a call on NTU research director David R. Keating. Keating is a short, slender man with a brown under-the-chin beard; if you were on the opposite end of Pennsylvania Avenue, you might mistake him for a drama student at George Washington University. He is intensely devoted to the cause of federal budget control, a cause which has brought him an intimate knowledge of the workings of the pork-barrel system.

"The trouble," he told me, "is that we've got all these spending interests—special-interest groups, state interests, whatever—and they're all lobbying hard for that one specific issue from which they'll get a lot of money. So it's a big deal with them, and they can put a great deal of effort into it. And on the other side, we've got the taxpayer, where it only costs them a nickel for something minor to a dollar, or whatever, for a larger project—and what you have is constantly the taxpayer coming out on the bottom. Because he doesn't have the resources, he doesn't have the clout— he doesn't really care enough to fight every nickel-and-dime thing that's proposed. And we see that as a fundamental defect in the system."

These sentiments are echoed elsewhere. "The typical situation of a pork-barrel project," Joel Aberbach emphasizes at the Brookings, "is that there's a group that's very anxious to have the project, and could benefit a great deal from it, and that most people are relatively indifferent." And a few blocks away, at Common Cause, lobbyist Jane Wishner makes the same point. ". . . there's a *lot* of public participation. My God, they fly in all the sixty farmers who'll benefit. But it's a question of the rest of us, who pay

the bill for it, and aren't really aware of it, or don't care."
The pork interests, by contrast, do care. They care very
much.

One Sunday afternoon in Washington shortly after talking with David Keating, I spent several hours running an
empirical test on the depth of that caring by wandering
about the city and looking at the buildings housing the
various elements of the pork lobby. Sometimes it seemed
that half of Washington must be constituted of these buildings. In addition to the National Chamber of Commerce in
its aforementioned neo-Corinthian heap on Lafayette
Square, there was the National Association of Manufacturers in its white marble monument nestled cozily between
the General Services Administration and the White House,
the coal industry associations in their black one near the
National Geographic Building, and the American Truckers'
Association in its pink one on P Street, just off Embassy
Row. There were the National Association of Dredging
Contractors and the National Association of River and Harbor Contractors in their upper-floor offices in the Washington Building, a tall granite spire which, symbolically or not,
hangs over the neighboring United States Treasury like the
sword of Damocles. There was the American Public Works
Association in its tall steel-and-glass building across from
the Brookings Institution, the American Road and Transportation Builders' Association in its strategically located
headquarters across from the Department of Transportation, and the superbly positioned National Water Resources Association on L'Enfant Plaza, some of the most
expensive real estate in Washington, a half-minute's stroll
from the Department of Transportation and just across the
George Mason Memorial Bridge from the Pentagon. There
were dozens—perhaps hundreds—of others.

By way of contrast, the public-interest lobbies (with a few
notable exceptions such as Common Cause, which occupies an entire floor of a modern office building in the bank-

ing district, near the American Petroleum Institute) always seem to be tucked away in threadbare little offices in obscure corners. The twin townhouses of the National Taxpayers' Union are atypical only in the fact that there are two of them and hence somewhat more space than usual, an advantage offset by the necessity of sharing space and staff with the Balance the Budget Amendment Committee. The Sierra Club occupies a musty, high-vaulted rabbit warren of ancient "temporary" partitions in what appears to be a converted ballroom in the old Naval Lodge Building near the Capitol. Across the street, the Environmental Policy Center and the League of Conservation Voters operate out of even tighter quarters in another converted townhouse, this one a two-story walkup above a Roy Rogers restaurant. On nearby C Street, Ralph Nader's Congress Watch holds down similar offices. The overwhelming impression one gets prowling back and forth between the two types of lobby is that of a small squadron of undernourished Davids going up against a superbly conditioned and equipped army of Goliaths.

Not only are the public-interest lobbyists outgunned and outmanned, but the rules are bent subtly against them as well. Internal Revenue regulations, for example, allow corporations to deduct the costs of lobbying from their taxes as a legitimate business expense. But any nonprofit organization which openly lobbies Congress can have its tax-exempt status removed, and donations to it cannot be deducted come April 15. Since most of the pork lobby is composed of profit-making corporations and most of the public-interest lobby is made up of nonprofit organizations, the effect of this pair of IRS regulations is to encourage lobbying for pork and discourage lobbying against it. It also means that a citizen who unsuccessfully fights a pork-barrel project will get stuck at least three times—once for the project itself, once for his lobbying costs against it and once for the pork lobby's lobbying costs *for* it, the last in the form of higher taxes to make up for the government's loss of revenue on all that money the pork lobby is paying to rob it blind—and then blissfully deducting from its taxes.

Because they have all that extra money—thanks, in part, to the largesse of the IRS—the pork lobby can afford to hire a fundamentally different kind of lobbyist. The difference involved has nothing to do with matters of talent, qualifications, or dedication, all of which both the pork and the public-interest lobby have in abundance. It is, instead, a caste distinction, as radical in its own way as the difference between Brahman and Untouchable in pre-Gandhi India.

There is in Washington a fairly large body of ex-senators and ex-representatives who currently serve as lobbyists. Along with the intangible but very real extra connections this gives them when they go to lobby their former comrades-in-arms comes a set of quite tangible extra privileges. The most important of these is the privilege of the floor in the body in which they formerly served. Only senators and ex-senators are allowed on the floor of the Senate, and only representatives and ex-representatives are allowed on the floor of the House. This means that these "ex"-lobbyists are allowed to continue applying pressure right into the House or Senate chamber while a vote is in progress, something no run-of-the-mill lobbyist could possibly hope to get away with. Such accessibility does not come cheap, and the financially strapped public-interest groups are uniformly outbid. As far as I have been able to determine, there is not a single public-interest lobby in Washington with one of these Brahman lobbyists on its payroll.

All of these things—more money, higher numbers, and accessibility—mean greater relative power for the pork lobby in the process of attempting to influence the nation's laws. But there is an even more fundamental distinction between the pork and public-interest lobbies, one that could not be erased even if by some miracle the public-interest lobbies were suddenly granted all the money and numbers and accessibility they wanted. It is a distinction that has to do with the basic orientation of the two lobbies toward the issues. Public-interest lobbies almost always are generalists. Pork lobbies almost always are not.

Public-interest lobbyists, almost by definition, are ideologues, and their presence in Washington is dedicated to furthering some ideological cause—lower taxes, clean government, a clean environment, world peace. This means that they must pay attention to a very broad range of legislation in an attempt to shape the nation's whole body of laws to conform to their ideology. The National Taxpayers' Union typifies this approach. "Our principal purpose is to reduce taxes and reduce government spending," NTU's David Keating told me. "We see it as our role to try and oppose spending projects wherever we feel we can make a dent. We try to take everything, although we don't have the resources. I think the best indication of how we take everything is our most recent voting study. It covers every vote last year that had *any* conceivable connection with spending money. Anything that was for spending money, or against reducing spending, we considered a negative vote."

A similar broad-brush approach will be found at the Sierra Club, which tries to keep track of everything that has any conceivable connection with the environment, or at Common Cause, which tries to keep track of everything that has any conceivable connection with a clean, open legislative process, or at the Friends' Committee on National Legislation (the so-called Quaker lobby), which tries to keep track of everything that has any conceivable connection with peace, humanitarianism, and social justice. Covering a ball park that big is obviously going to spread a team rather thin, no matter how big the team is and how quick their outfielders are.

The pork lobby, on the other hand, is often tightly focused on specific points of law. There are ideologically related pork lobbies—the National Association of Manufacturers, the National Alliance of Businessmen, the National Chamber of Commerce—but they are outnumbered by a plethora of true special-interest lobbies with extremely limited fields of concern. A glance at a list of lobby names will quickly confirm this. Lobbying offices are maintained in Washington by the National Association of Margarine Manufacturers, the National Association of Chain Drug Stores, the National Association of Metal Name Plate Manufacturers, and the National Association of Minority Certified Public Accountant Firms, to name but a few. The National American Indian Court Judges Association has an active lobby, as does the National Association for Women Deans, Administrators, and Counselors, and the National Association of State Savings and Loan Supervisors. The list goes on and on, and it adds up to a collection of many intense, localized points of pressure, each of which is free to put its whole effort into lobbying within its tiny and highly specific field of interest. Trying to oppose this approach with the broad-field tactics of the public-interest lobbies is a little like trying to stop a cat fight by covering it with cellophane. You may have enough material to cover the field, but the cats have the strength to break through at just about any point they choose.

The result of this issue-specific pressure—"endless pressure, endlessly applied," in the favorite phrase of Sierra Club head lobbyist Brock Evans—is often an incredible free ride for some special interest at taxpayer expense. Some examples:

- *Waterway users' fees.* There are more than 25,000 miles of inland waterways in the United States, most of them built, maintained, and operated by the federal government. Barge companies have traditionally used federal waterways at no charge, a practice which amounted to a gigantic federal subsidy for the barge industry (imagine a 25,000-mile railway system built, operated, and maintained by taxpayers' money and used by railway companies free of charge, or a 25,000-mile federally built highway system on which truckers were exempt from license fees, gasoline taxes, and weight/mile charges). Every president from Franklin Roosevelt through Gerald Ford tried to get waterway users' fees instituted, but the barge lobby successfully fought off all their attempts. Then Jimmy Carter tried, and he succeeded—after a fashion. A users' fee was finally signed into law in 1978. But it is a wishywashy users' fee, a fee which the Environmental Policy Center's Brent Blackwelder charges will only pay for between 5 and 10 percent of the cost of the waterways to the taxpayer. The barge lobby lost on paper, but it is crying all the way to the bank.

- *Cost sharing.* The barge companies' free ride on federal waterways is typical of public works in the water field, where the chief beneficiaries of a given project almost never pay any part of its costs. This seems grossly unfair. Cost sharing, in which those who benefit from a project would be required to pay part of its costs, would eliminate much of this unfairness. This reasoning has made cost sharing a key portion of President Carter's attempted water policy reform, where it has been endorsed by everyone from the army's Don Dillon ("I think the president's cost-sharing proposal is the very best part of his water policy reform: we've recommended it in all the reports we've submitted to Congress recently") to the Environmental Policy Center's Brent Blackwelder ("We've long supported full recovery of the costs of water projects from the beneficiaries of such projects. If the beneficiaries had to pay, then the pressure for many unsound projects would vanish"). President Carter has submitted legislation to Congress nearly every year since his election to establish extremely low-level cost sharing, on the order of 5 to 10 percent of project costs. Every year, a coalition of irrigation lobbyists and local government lobbies has defeated it.
- *Cost overruns.* Even when reasonable cost sharing is hammered into a public-works bill, cost overruns, typically

borne entirely by the government, often skew the results entirely out of shape. The Clinch River Breeder Reactor project is a splendid (or terrible) example. "That started out as 50/50 funding between government and industry," complains NTU's David Keating. "It's now over 88 percent taxpayers and only 12 percent industry, because industry has refused to raise its contribution to the project. On the other hand, they're still lobbying for it like crazy." And why not? With a deal like that going for them, the chance to build something whose real costs have more than quadrupled without affecting their costs by so much as a penny, they'd be crazy not to lobby.

● *Free use of government production facilities.* When a contractor gets a construction contract from the government, the pork doesn't end there. Often he gets to use the government's own facilities to do the construction. A 1960 study by the Friends' Committee on National Legislation found that "producers of military hardware are almost uniformly allowed to use federal plants and equipment free of charge. . . . Boeing's profit in 1958 was based upon a private investment of $145 million and $245 million of government facilities; Douglas' profit was based upon a private capital investment of $123 million and a gross government investment of $215 million. . . ." The study went on to list similar spending patterns for Lockheed, North American, and the Martin Company. The twenty years since have seen no real change in this pattern, which, needless to say, has been intensively lobbied for by the aerospace industry.

How do the lobbies engineer these free rides at public expense? Sometimes the tactics employed are rather shady, as in the case of California's New Melones Dam. When the dam was brought to a statewide vote, the prodam lobby ran a massive billboard campaign with such a misleading message that, when contacted after the vote, 58 percent of those who had voted for the dam complained that they thought they were voting against it (the billboard campaign was later discovered to have been bankrolled by a contribution of $175,000 from the contractor who was building the dam).

Sometimes the tactics are downright illegal, as in the several cases where unethical lobbyists have been discovered running phony angry-constituent campaigns. In a typical case reported in Neil MacNeill's *Forge of Democracy*, utility companies opposed to a public-utilities regulation bill before Congress in 1935 were found to be flooding Capitol Hill with as many as 4,000 telegrams per hour signed with names picked at random from telephone directories and used without their owners' knowledge or consent.

But though these are the cases that make headlines, they are far from typical. The normal lobbyist is a hard-working, diligent, honest individual whose main tools are a fine grasp of political procedures, an intimate knowledge of the subject under consideration, and a firm belief that the government owes him something. His principal function is to serve as a storehouse of facts, and to use those facts to persuade congressmen to vote the way he wants them to. Most of his work is not done in the Capitol building lobbies from which he gets his name, but in the cavernous marble corridors of the House and Senate office buildings, where he may be seen trudging from office to office with his portfolios and his fact sheets, arguing, cajoling, and occasionally enlightening the congressmen, senators, and aides he comes into contact with. He keeps lists of those who are for him, against him, and on the fence, normally filing the first two groups of names and concentrating on the third, where there is still some chance of changing minds. To some extent he serves as an errand boy and a messenger service, coordinating the congressmen who agree with him, informing them when key votes are coming up, keeping the information and the communication flowing among their offices. Often he writes the legislation which the congressman will later introduce as his own, not because he has worked some shady deal but because the congressman and his staff simply don't have enough hours in the day to do everything that needs to be done. The writing of legislation is a task that the lobbyist, with his detailed knowledge of the proposed law's subject matter, seems ideally qualified to lift from their shoulders. In fact, he does so many things of so much importance that it is probably no exaggeration to say that Congress would come to a screeching halt without him. Legislation in the United States depends heavily on the lobbies. It is not far removed from the model suggested by American Legion lobbyist John Thomas Taylor, who remarked in a disgruntled mood in 1953 that "legislation is literally made outside the halls of Congress by groups of persons interested in legislation, mainly with economic motives, and the deliberative process within Congress constitutes a sort of formal ratification."

But if the lobbyist is indispensible, it does not follow that he is also omnipotent. The pork lobbyist is necessary for the maintainance of the pork-barrel system, but he cannot hold it up alone. He needs help. Often he gets some of that help from the federal bureaucracy. Sometimes he gets most of it there.

Bureaucrats are indispensable to the pork-barrel system for the simple reason that once a program is porked into place, it is the bureaucrats and their agencies who will be responsible for carrying it out: building the dam, administering the grant, enforcing the tariff, whatever. Since *building, administering, enforcing,* and most of the other words for what bureaucrats do are all in some sense passive, implying reaction rather than action—a mere follow-through of decisions reached elsewhere—bureau personnel will usually tell you that pork barreling is not their fault, because they only do what Congress tells them to do. "I agree with you. I don't like the present system," one major agency head told me sincerely. "But I recognize their prerogatives." This, unfortunately, is an exact analog of the plaintive cry of Gestapo officers at Nuremberg: "I was only following orders!" It is comforting to have the responsibility for your actions rest on someone else's shoulders, but it is not very realistic. The orders may come from Congress, but they do not spring to life there by spontaneous generation. Someone has to have provided the data, outlined the alternatives, and supplied the rationale upon which the orders are based; and as often as not the providers, outliners, and suppliers turn out to be the agencies themselves.

Congressmen perpetuate the pork-barrel system for reasons that have largely to do with self-preservation. If they do enough for their districts, the voters will return them to office. ("It's the old Edifice Complex," says George Pring dryly. "That's how you get reelected.") The agencies hold down their corner of the Iron Triangle for similar motives. Government agencies are almost always mission-oriented. They have a role to fill, and if the reason for that role disappears the agency will disappear right along with it. If an agency's mission is to build dams, it must continue to find new dams to build; if its mission is to dispense grants, then it must find grantees to dispense them to; if its mission is to defend against enemy attack, then it must find both an enemy (hence the staunch anticommunism and rabid cold-war mentality of most military personnel) and a means of defense (new, better, and more weapons systems, military bases, communications and warning devices, and so forth). Nobody likes to work himself out of a job, and bureaucrats are no different from the rest of us on that account. Nor is this attitude particularly wrong—as an attitude. It is only when it gets mistaken for a rationale and plugged into that lower left-hand corner of the Iron Triangle, where it can be propped up by similar attitudes in the other two corners, that the trouble begins.

In Denver, George Pring talks about the Bureau of Reclamation. "You know," he says, "water politics here in the West is almost inseparable from the pork barrel. But that's not an indictment of the system. The system that developed was really very necessary, and at first it worked probably more effectively than any other water system ever could. You see, in this area, there isn't enough rainfall to start with, and to make matters worse it all falls in the form of snow or rain in a very short period of time. It has to be caught in order to space it out over an agricultural growing season of one hundred eight days, let alone be able to provide a municipality or an industry that needs twelve-months-a-year, regular flows of water. Storage, then, immediately becomes the name of the game.

"But as soon as people discovered, about the time of Teddy Roosevelt, that they could give away all the land that they wanted to out here but nobody in their right minds would come settle it without water-storage facilities, they also discovered that those facilities would require a considerably greater investment than most private individuals, or even groups of private individuals, could put in. And so in 1902 the feds moved in with the Federal Reclamation Act —a very enlightened piece of *public-works,* as opposed to *pork-barrel,* legislation, in those days—which enabled the federal government to build and subsidize and operate storage facilities for water to encourage development in the Western expansion. Otherwise we might be sitting in an outpost of Mexico or Russia today. I don't know which one would have won, or even wanted it, without the water.

"The problem, though, is that basically by World War Two all of the worthwhile projects had already been built, and even a number of near-worthwhile ones had already been built—if we take 'worthwhile projects' to mean those which allow good agricultural or municipal or industrial development, where the costs and benefits are at least in some sort of balance. What we're into now, in current times, is absolutely scraping the bottom of the pork barrel.

It's not just pork barreling. We're into the 'pits projects,' the projects that no sane engineer with even one course in economics can recommend without getting a crinkly smile on his face. Unless, of course, he's a federal bureaucrat, and the continuation of his agency is absolutely dependent upon the building of that project. And that's what's happened to the Bureau of Reclamation and its original 1902 mission."

Some of what Pring refers to as the Bureau of Reclamation's "pits projects" are so incredible as to almost defy belief. It is the Bureau, for example, that wants to dam Grand Canyon—not because it thinks the water is needed (the Colorado River is drastically overappropriated anyway), but because it wants to generate power to sell to raise revenue that can be used to build more projects elsewhere. It is the Bureau that is pushing the Garrison Diversion Project, which will take 220,000 acres of North Dakota farmland out of production in order to irrigate another 250,000 acres which is mostly already producing and doesn't need the irrigation anyway. (When one farmer, Ben Schatz, objected to his land being taken for Garrison, Bureau officials told him, "To us you're just a dot on the map. When you get in the way, we move you." Schatz subsequently erected a gigantic billboard: "My farm ruined by the U.S. Bureau of Reclamation.")

It is the Bureau that wants to spend three quarters of a billion dollars of your money to take 300,000 acre-feet of water per year out of the Colorado River basin, where the water is already so overused that the Colorado won't flow into the Gulf of California unless Bureau engineers let it, and pour it into Great Salt Lake. (All right, I'm oversimplifying, and I admit it. The water would be used by residents of Salt Lake City first. But there is no real proof that Salt Lake City needs the water, except to maintain the kind of water-profligate life style which may be appropriate to the rainy Northeast but is extremely out of place out in the middle of the Great American Desert. And if it does, the Bureau is not the appropriate agency to supply it, because its legislatively defined mission is to reclaim agricultural land, not build city water systems. And the water *would* eventually end up in the lake, which scares the pants off most scientists. What will Great Salt Lake do with 300,000 extra acre-feet of water per year? No one knows.)

Finally, it was the Bureau which built Teton Dam, whose eventual collapse was predicted several years prior to construction by numerous geologists, including a team from the U.S. Geological Survey, which concluded in a memo following its study that if the Bureau went ahead and built the dam the Survey "might consider a series of strategically placed motion picture cameras to document the progress of catastrophic flooding." All of these projects, and many others which could be cited, fit quite clearly into the Bureau's "pits projects" category.

In order to support these questionable endeavors, the Bureau of Reclamation and the other agencies which commonly pull projects out of the pits utilize a variety of gamesmanship techniques, many of which are strongly tied in with the pork-barrel syndrome. The Department of Defense and its overextended network of military bases ("They've all been there since the Civil War or before," complains Tom Dine of the Brookings, "and they just keep going"), the Department of Agriculture and its masses of research grants which have proved, among other things, that most women don't like to iron and that most consumers prefer fresh tomatoes (except, perhaps, to throw at officials like the one who authorized the study), the Department of State and its little group of offices which were set up to protect the Western Hemisphere against Nazi invasion in World War II but were at last report still going their quietly irrelevant way on our money more than thirty years after the close of hostilities—all these hook up to the pork barrel.

The reasons for this tie-in are not too difficult to discover. In order to sneak a padded budget through Congress, an agency needs a good congressional image, and there are few better ways to achieve such an image than to help individual lawmakers get reelected. Conversely, if an agency feels that it needs to get tough with Congress to force through an appropriation that is clearly opposed by the majority of lawmakers, the best place to apply pressure is the place where it will hurt the most—a one-two punch right in the old electorate. The agencies, in other words, can manipulate Congress to a surprisingly large degree by either supplying or withholding pork, whichever seems more appropriate, and any high-level bureaucrat worth his salt is equally adept at both.

Sometimes, to be sure, this does no harm. If the Forest Service can build a needed tree nursery anywhere in a two-state area, to pick one recent example, it hurts no one to let them gain a few points by locating it in the district of the chairman of the House Agriculture Committee's Subcommittee on Forestry. If a grant-giving agency such as the National Endowment for the Humanities assures passage of its budget by making certain that its grants go to as many congressional districts as possible, this may bloat the agency's budget a bit, but it is certainly better than the alternative of placing all the grants in one or two key districts and ignoring all the others. As Common Cause's Jane Wishner puts it, "The question is, should all the good projects be in the districts of the committee chairs, or should they be distributed more across the country?" Given a choice, most people would undoubtedly opt for the latter. If the problems with pork barreling are problems of inequitable resource distribution—and many of them are—this is certainly one way to go about solving them. "As long as the essential purpose of the program is not perverted," points out Aaron Wildavsky, "fitting the activity to the need for widespread constituency support increases an important value in a democratic society—consent. Surely, a program like summer institutes for mathematics teachers is not rendered less desirable by being distributed in a good many constituencies." Looked at that way, what appears to be massive pork barreling may actually turn out to be pork-barrel reform.

On the other hand, much agency manipulation of Congress is not nearly so innocuous. The problems of pork barreling are not all concerned with resource distribution. Some of them are concerned with resource misallocation, or sheer, unadulterated waste, and in these cases spreading things around more evenly is not going to help very much. If a program is a bust in one constituency, spreading it around to a lot of constituencies is not going to make it any less of a bust—just a bust that is more certain to be enacted. A needless expenditure does not automatically become needed by making sure that everybody gets a piece of it. "Used to be," laments one top-echelon agency official who prefers to remain nameless, "we could dole out the pork to fifteen committee chairmen and get our program through. Now, with all the reforms that have gone in recently, we've got to hand something out to all four hundred thirty-five congressmen. It's given pork barreling a vast new lease on life."

The methods that agencies use to manipulate Congress can be remarkably brazen. There is, for example, a technique known as phased buying, where Congress gives an agency the funds to buy x number of widgets and the agency uses the money instead to buy twice that number of partial widgets, forcing Congress to appropriate enough money to buy the rest of each widget before any of them can go into operation. The air force once used phased buying almost routinely for its weapons contracts. It was

called on the carpet in 1957 by Defense Secretary Charles
Wilson and ordered to desist, and no agency has openly
practiced the method since. But vestiges of it remain in
such practices as budgetary underestimating. Naval programs, for example, continually show cost overruns of 100
percent, which means that the navy's budgetary officers are
continually underestimating costs by a factor of 50 percent.
That in turn means that they are either grossly incompetent
or are doing it on purpose.

Another variant on phased buying is incremental budgeting (a Corps of Engineers favorite). Incremental budgeting
involves placing a very small amount of money into an
agency's annual budget to begin what will eventually be a
multimillion-dollar program. The budgetary item can be
defended on the grounds that it is, say, "just $5,000," but
the agency is well aware that once Congress has made that
token commitment of funds it will be extremely difficult to
justify backing out—and "wasting" the money—when two
years later a request comes in for $20 million to finish what
the $5,000 started.

Then there is information manipulation. Since the
agency is always the principal, and often the sole, source of
information about its programs, Congress usually gets a
distorted view of how efficient and valuable the programs
are, or even of what their real nature may be. "If the president comes out with an environmental message, you begin
to reclassify all the programs you can as 'environmental'
and beef them up," an agency budget official told author
Leonard Reed. "We call the guys who work in cost/benefit
analysis the 'fix-it shop,' " one Corps district employee acknowledged to me quite frankly, adding that they were
expected to be able to make just about any project the
Corps wanted to build appear feasible.

There is also direct political pressure, applied through a
vast network of agency "congressional liaison officers" who
together form a lobby once characterized by Lambert

Miller of the National Association of Manufacturers as "the most pervasive, influential and costly of any such in the whole country." (At last report there were more than five hundred of these agency flacks prowling the halls of Congress, or about one "liaison officer" for every member of Congress that needed liaison.)

Last but hardly least, there is a technique which we will refer to as the "manipulation of constituent pressure." This technique is a bit tricky to use, but, once mastered, is probably the most effective of all. Instead of putting pressure on a congressman, the agency practicing constituent-opinion manipulation puts pressure on the congressman's constituents. The difficulty of this technique is that it may take the agency a while to find the right button. The beauty, though, is that once you have pushed that button you can sit back and relax, because the pork ethic will do the rest of your work for you.

Consider this chain of events. The year is 1962, the space program is struggling to get off the ground, the national debt is a staggering but still manageable $303 billion, and President Kennedy is seeking permission from Congress to raise it to $308 billion. Congress is dragging its heels. 1962 is an election year, and the members know what the public will say to $5 billion more in deficit spending. Or do they? Aha! Someone in the administration—perhaps a presidential advisor, perhaps some high-level bureaucrat in the Pentagon, perhaps Jack Kennedy himself—gets an idea. Soon little notes are going out from the Pentagon to virtually every defense contractor in the nation: Sorry, boys, but unless this bill raising the national debt goes through there won't be enough money in the Treasury to pay you. A damburst of mail pours onto an astonished Congress, from the defense contractors themselves, from workers who are afraid they'll be laid off, and from city governments and chambers of commerce in defense-industry communities all across the nation. The congressmen see through it, of course; "I say it smacks of blackmail!" shouts an angry John Byrnes of Wisconsin during floor debate in the House. But they also realize that there is no way they can fight it. Constituent pressure is constituent pressure, and no matter what force pulled the cork on the letter-bottle, the letters that are pouring out of it are genuine. The debt bill passes handily.

Other than the scope of the bill involved (affecting not just one agency but potentially all aspects of government operation), there is nothing particularly unusual about this story. All agencies have become adept at practicing manipulation of constituent opinion, what Aaron Wildavsky calls the "creative arrangement of clientele." Most employ "public information officers," full-time bureaucrats whose job is to go out into the community to build support for what the agency wants to do, through press releases, speeches to the Rotary, and so forth. Variations on the omnibus-bill approach are practiced, with programs designed to appeal to as broad a constituency as possible, as in the National Endowment for the Humanities example cited earlier. Or consider the Census Bureau's National Housing Inventory, redesigned (from an earlier housing-survey failure) to concentrate on developing information which would be useful primarily to groups such as local construction industries and retail trade associations, whose members were likely to write to their congressmen.

Often parts of a program will be carefully structured to fit a particular constituency. The Corps of Engineers is particularly good at this. Their standard approach is to come into an area, hold a series of "informational meetings" to sound out the local populace, and then design their projects to fit what those meetings show the population wants instead of solely what their engineering surveys show that it needs. It is an approach that pays off. When the Corps was designing southern Oregon's Applegate Dam, for example, they took public-opinion soundings in the three counties traversed by the Applegate River—Siskiyou in California and Jackson and Josephine in Oregon—and determined that (a) Siskiyou County and the state of California didn't want the dam at all; (b) Jackson County, which contained most of the river's course and all of the logical damsites, was lukewarm; and (c) Josephine County, with the river's mouth and lowest few miles, was ecstatic about the idea. The Corps' original plans had called for a dam that would have backed water nearly a mile into California up two separate streams. With the results of the survey in hand, they redesigned it, bringing it downstream a half-mile and lowering its crest, so that the high-water mark on the reservoir was precisely on the state line. That took care of the opposition in California. They then proceeded to hold virtually all remaining public meetings on the dam in Josephine County, where support was strong, rather than in Jackson County, where support was lukewarm—even though their own engineering work showed that the dam would have only minimal effects in Josephine County but would highly impact Jackson County. The result was an appearance of extraordinarily strong support for a dam whose backing was really rather weak, and whose rationale was almost totally nonexistent.

Occasionally, in attempting to demonstrate public support for its programs, an agency will get downright shady. This was the case with the Forest Service's RARE II program in the winter of 1978–1979. RARE II, briefly stated, was a study designed to determine how much Forest Service land should be used for timber production and how much should be recommended for congressional designation as wilderness. The process included a healthy solicitation of public opinion, which the agency specifically requested to take the form of personal letters only. Multiple copies of form letters and multiple signatures on petitions, they said, would not be counted. Unfortunately, when the input showed up, those personal letters turned out to be heavily weighted in favor of substantially more wilderness than the agency wanted to be stuck with. Their solution? Change the guidelines for public input *after the input was in.* Form letters and petitions, they decided, should be counted after all. It was no coincidence that those form letters and petitions came almost exclusively from the timber industry, which had not been following the guidelines from the beginning, and which enjoys a close symbiotic relationship with the Forest Service throughout most of the West. (In Texas, for example, the regional forester, the man in charge of all national forests in the state, was also the chairman of the industry's lobbying organization.) As a result of this conscious manipulation of data, the Forest Service was able in some cases to precisely reverse the public-input count, going from two-thirds in favor of wilderness for a given area to two-thirds in favor of logging the same piece of land.

In order to demonstrate constituent support, the agencies depend heavily on the lobbies, and it is this heavy dependence which forms the broad, stable base of the Iron Triangle. The bond between the lobbies and the agencies is cemented by a number of practices, the most pernicious of which is probably that of crossover employment—the hiring of agency personnel by industries whose income is dependent on the actions of that agency. Crossover employment is practiced by all agencies. A 1962 study by Lester W. Milbraith found that 57 out of 114 lobbyists questioned, precisely one-half, had come to their lobby employment directly from government service either in the executive or legislative branch.

Crossover employment is probably worst among former employees of the military and the Corps of Engineers, who have engaged in it since their establishment. In fact, Corps officials once made a common practice of simultaneous crossover employment, hiring themselves out to the civilian contractors who were working on their projects while they were still on the Corps payroll. This practice was legislatively halted by Congress in 1838. Since then, legal crossover employment has been solely sequential. It has not, however, significantly diminished. In Oklahoma, the head of the Port of Tulsa is a former Corps employee; in Arkansas, the chairman of the Brazos River Authority has, as the army's Don Dillon puts it discreetly, "retired from the Corps." In Oregon, Colonel Paul Triem helped plan Lost Creek Dam on the Rogue River in his position as head of the Corps' Portland District, then resigned to join the staff of the Umpqua River Navigation Company. The Umpqua River Navigation Company subsequently built Lost Creek Dam. The list goes on and on.

Military connections are similar. A 1959 study by a special subcommittee of the House Armed Services Committee found that 80 percent of the government's arms business was going to a few large aerospace firms who had hired, among them, a total of 285 generals and admirals and more than 400 other officers above the rank of colonel. One company alone—General Dynamics Corporation, at that time the nation's number-one defense contractor—employed 186 retired officers, including 20 admirals and 7 generals; its chairman of the board, Frank Pace, was a former secretary of the army. There is no real evidence that this situation has improved. A cross-check between the 1978 editions of *Who's Who in America* and *Moody's Industrial Directory* indicates that General Dynamics—still number one in military sales, pulling in 7 percent of 1978's defense-industry dollars—is still top-heavy with former military officers and agency personnel (its executive vice-president for aerospace, for example, is a former administrator of the National Aeronautics and Space Administration).

Government officials tend to discount crossover employment as natural and proper, no different than any other change of jobs. "That's right," admits Dillon, "the Corps people go to the lobby groups and the lobbyists go to the

Corps. But I don't think there's necessarily anything bad about that." Perhaps not; but it does make for a suspiciously cozy arrangement. The ex-agency employee is not going to drop off the face of the earth as far as his friends in the office are concerned just because he is no longer working with them. They are going to continue to exchange Christmas cards, have lunch together, watch each other's kids grow up, and generally relate on far closer terms than can possibly be achieved by someone who simply walks off the street into one of the agency's offices. In governmentese, this is called "access," and it is extremely important. It is access that builds the close cooperation between the lobbies and the agencies that forms the operating base of the Iron Triangle, and it is access as much as expertise that the companies are buying when they hire these people. The chairman of the House Armed Services special subcommittee which commissioned the 1959 study, Representative F. Edward Hebert of Louisiana, acknowledged this when he reported the results of the study to his colleagues in the House. He was, he said, "not quite satisfied that all of the salaries [of the retired officers employed by defense contractors] were associated with pious hard work. The coincidence of increased company business and the employment of retired officers may have been accidental but it left me skeptical." Hebert, it should be noted, was no enemy of the Pentagon; if he is skeptical, so should we all be.

Perhaps the worst form of crossover employment is the form generally known as the "revolving-door syndrome," in which an individual leaves a private company for government service and then returns to the company several years later. A splendid example of this surfaced in a Ralph Nader Study Group publication called *The Monopoly Makers* in 1973, also involving General Dynamics. The company, it seems, had an attorney named Roswell Gilpatrick, who left it to become deputy secretary of defense for a while and

then came back to his old job. In the interim, General
Dynamics had won several juicy defense plums, including
the coveted TFX missile contract. Was this coincidence? A
Senate investigating committee didn't think so. They labeled it a "flagrant conflict of interest." Nader's group was
more cautious, merely referring to it as a "facile exchange
of personnel." A bit too facile for belief, perhaps, unless
you also believe in Santa Claus, the tooth fairy, and the
Dow Jones industrial averages.

Along with the exchange of personnel between lobbies
and agencies goes a substantial exchange of information.
Cooperation is extremely close on "problems of mutual
interest"—i.e., programs or projects which the agency
would like to see instituted and which local lobbies see as
particularly beneficial to their members. Sometimes this is
relatively innocuous. Agency personnel are featured speak-
ers and "honored guests" at lobby-group meetings, lobbies and agencies show up on each other's mailing lists,
interest groups are allowed free access to agency files,
agencies receive regular briefings on local news events
which might help sway a recalcitrant congressman.

At other times, though (and all too often), the cooperation tends to be considerably less above-board. Agencies
may make a surface appearance of going along with presidential directives for economy in a certain policy area, but
feed lobby groups reams of information concerning the
projects that they would really like to be doing, projects
which the lobbying group will then present before Congress as their own ideas while the agency is able to sit in the
back of the room nodding its head and saying, "Yes, we
could do that, if the president would let us." The lobbies
and the agencies may hold joint strategy sessions to determine the best way to influence Congress. Sometimes the
local congressman or one of his representatives will be in
on these sessions as well. Opponents of the agencies' plans
often find it suspiciously difficult to come up with relatively

routine information which the lobbies who favor the plans can waltz away with as a matter of course. In one case of this type in which I was involved, a group of us advocating the creation of a wilderness area on Forest Service land in southern Oregon and northern California found it infernally difficult to get on National Forest timber-sale mailing lists. It took two requests to get on one list, three to get on another, four—and the threat of a lawsuit—on a third. Any logging contractor, of course, could have found his way onto any of those lists with ease.

Internal memos may be leaked to lobby groups which can make the best use of them. Field offices may break ranks with headquarters in Washington, actively supporting pork-barrel schemes which the administration has come out against and which the upper-echelon personnel therefore feel duty-bound to oppose as well. After President Carter issued his famous "hit list" of irresponsible water projects in 1977, Corps of Engineers headquarters in Washington gave him token support while several field offices around the country actively passed out propaganda in favor of killing the hit list and retaining the projects. In the most notorious of these cases, the Corps' Missouri office openly defied the hit list and mounted a full-scale campaign to save the Meremec Park project, even though Missouri voters had just rejected it overwhelmingly in a statewide referendum.

In some even more suspicious cases, agency personnel have turned up as officers in lobby groups. And there has been at least one, and probably several, instances of agency personnel coopting an organization which might normally be expected to oppose its projects by getting its own people elected to the organization's board of directors and then proceeding to make policy their way. Instead of fighting the local Isaac Walton League chapter over a dam in one Western state, the Corps and its supporting lobbies merely infiltrated it; as soon as they had a majority on the executive committee, they rammed through a resolution in favor of the dam. The national Walton League office disowned that support, but the damage had been done. To this day, most people in the vicinity of the completed dam believe that it went in with the full blessings of the normally antidam "Ikeys."

Few of the practices that I have just listed—perhaps none of them—are actually illegal. Furthermore, none by itself is even particularly obnoxious. It is even possible to defend some of them on the grounds that they are part of the job —keeping the local populace informed and cooperating with local governments (who are often well represented on these interest-group boards). The agencies can also point, quite righteously, to a certain impartiality. They give speeches to project opponents as well as project supporters, they comply with the Freedom of Information Act in keeping their files available to anyone who wishes to walk into the office and use them, and they are quite adept at maintaining good relations all around. The problem is not with the techniques (though I suspect that we could do without several of them quite nicely). The problem is with the cumulative results that these techniques are able to achieve when thrust into the sturdy framework of the Iron Triangle and combined with similar activities in the other two corners. It is not the zeal with which agencies go about defending their programs that is wrong, but the unholy alliance of that zeal with the lobbyists' self-interest and the congressman's pork ethic. As long as Congress remains convinced that the agencies' grand schemes to promote the special interests' welfare are just what the constituents want, we're going to continue to have problems. And to the extent that the attitudes and activities of the agencies contribute to the continuation of that nasty little three-cornered cycle, the agencies are part of those problems.

Agencies are not always to blame for pork. The Iron

Triangle is not totally unassailable; breakdowns do occur, and when they do the agency corner is usually the one that collapses. When the Corps wants the Cross-Florida Barge Canal deauthorized, and Congress refuses to push the right buttons, it is hardly the Corps' fault. When the air force wants to close Loring, or the navy wants to avoid buying useless destroyers, or the Weather Bureau wants to close the Mt. Sexton Weather Station, it is certainly wrong to accuse the agencies of wallowing in the pork when the money for these things gets spent over their objections. "A lot of times writers will criticize the agencies for pork barreling, but in many cases it's local lobby pressures stopping a cost-effective move of one form or another," points out Tom Dine of the Brookings.

Even when they appear to be going along, the agencies will sometimes have their feet stuck out of the rolling pork barrel, attempting to slow it down and to keep it from juggernauting all vestiges of common sense. Occasionally they get caught at it, as in this Senate Appropriations Committee hearings dialogue, reported by John Ferejohn, between General Itschner of the Corps of Engineers and a certain Northwest senator whom Ferejohn identifies only as "Senator X" over the issue of full funding (obtaining all the money for a given project at once instead of in yearly increments):

GENERAL ITSCHNER: What I am proposing is that for construction projects we would come to you just once for a single appropriation.

　　　If we needed more money later, if we could not do the job for the amount of money that we originally said we would require, then we would have to come before you to explain why, and obtain an additional appropriation. . . .

SENATOR X: Are you suggesting a lump-sum appropriation for a project such as John Day Dam, that cost how much?

GENERAL ITSCHNER: $418 million or something like that.

SENATOR X: Talk about shouting pork barrel, you would really get it there, I guess. That would make the initiation of a large project almost impossible.

GENERAL ITSCHNER: This is just a suggestion. I recognize that disadvantage. . . . There are many disadvantages to it, but in the end I think it would save money. I recognize there are problems in doing it. But after the first year or two, after the system was put into effect, the overall bill should be no greater than it is now.

SENATOR X: I understand that, but without having studied the matter too deeply, I feel that the public reaction to a request for say a tenth or a fifth of the total cost of a project is bad enough, without going into this. . . . I believe that it would be much more difficult to obtain the funds for new starts under that system than under the present method.

The bureaucrats are not always the villains of the piece. Sometimes, as in General Itschner's valiant attempt to convince Congress that it was spending too much on his agency, they fight right along with the public-interest groups for lower budgets and less pork. As Don Dillon put it toward the close of our conversation, "I feel that if federal funds are going to be invested in a public-works project, then there should be some return to the national government. I no more than you want my tax dollars going to somebody in another state for something in which there's no benefit that anybody can describe that would return to me." Bureaucrats are taxpayers, too, and they don't appreciate seeing their money wasted any more than anyone else. They are likely to insist, in Dillon's terms, that "benefits accrue to the national account," and their insistence is honest, forthright, and vigorous.

Having said that, though, I think it is also fair to say that what agency personnel see as "benefits" are often quite different, and a lot more loosely defined, than what are seen as benefits by the rest of us. And the agencies are remarkably adept at finding these "benefits" in any project which they happen, for whatever reason, to want to do. Every agency has a fix-it shop, and most of them work overtime, not devising projects which meet desired criteria but devising criteria which desired projects can meet. For the overwhelming majority of cases, the Triangle—agency, lobby, congressman—is complete, active, and sturdy. Sturdier, in fact, than many of the projects that will result from its application. Agencies are not vicious, but they are self-righteous. And the fruits of that self-righteousness, the fruits of the pork barrel, roll on and on.

One of the more annoying characteristics of the Iron Triangle is that it is so deeply internalized. The lines of mutual support that develop between its three corners act like stone walls, shutting out the rest of the world; for the project in question, the Triangle becomes the world. It is nice and tight, combining the desire for something (the lobby), the ability to provide it (the agency), and the ability to pay for it (Congress), and to those closed within the lines there seems no need to look beyond them. Ties of camaraderie develop along with the ties of support. At the appropriations hearings each spring, the agencies, lobbies, and congressmen greet each other like long-lost friends; there is much mutual back-slapping and cross-congratulating, much admiration expressed for the agencies' "professionalism," the lobbyists' "dedication" and "community spirit," the congressman's "generosity" and "support." A class-reunion atmosphere pervades much of the hearings record, as in the following statement by Senator J. Bennett Johnston of Louisiana as a lobby delegation from his state trooped up to the witness table during the April 1978 hearings on the Public Works Appropriations Bill for Fiscal Year 1979:

SENATOR JOHNSTON. Now, we are glad to welcome our friend Herbert Haar, Sam Giallanza, senior vice-president of the

New Orleans Steamship Association, who has been with us for a number of years. Also Captain Daniel R. Meyers, president of the Associated Branch Pilots, and Jerry Dyson who is back again.

Very glad to have you, captain. You are always welcome here. He steers us right. [Laughter]

Or this exchange between John F. Stroud of the Red River Commission and Senator—formerly Governor—Dale Bumpers of Arkansas:

MR. STROUD. . . . I represent the Red River Commission of Arkansas that was created by the foresight of Governor Dale Bumpers.

SENATOR BUMPERS. I thought you would never get around to it. [Laughter]

Both Mr. Stroud and Mr. Haar and company were lucky enough to be addressing a Senate committee on which a senator from their own state was sitting. It is not necessary to be so blessed to take advantage of the hail-fellow-well-met conviviality within the Triangle, however. If your senator or congressman isn't on the committee, you can usually get him to come up to the witness table with you and tell all his friends on the committee what a good fellow you are.

SENATOR STENNIS. Gentlemen, this brings our subcommittee to the Falls Lake project in North Carolina. . . . I want to recognize Senator Jesse Helms who is here to testify. We want to know his reasons. We will be glad to hear from him now. . . .

SENATOR HELMS. Mr. Chairman, we will be very brief. Of course, it is always a pleasure to appear before any committee chaired by the distinguished senator from Mississippi. It is even more a pleasure to serve on the Armed Services Committee with him. He is a great American.

First of all, may I present some good friends of mine

from North Carolina: Mr. Ronald Earl Mason, representing the governor of North Carolina, James Hunt; L. P. Zachary, who is the city manager of my home city of Raleigh; W. H. Carper, who is the former city manager of Raleigh—and incidentally, I served on the city council while Mr. Carper was city manager.

SENATOR STENNIS. The two of you served together?

SENATOR HELMS. Yes, sir; Mr. Carper and I. Mr. Carper is now retired. As I look at his youthful appearance I think he must have retired at the age of thirty-nine. He is now associated with the Raleigh Chamber of Commerce and the Neuse River Basin Association.

On my right is Earl Bardin, a longtime friend, president of the Chamber of Commerce; Don Beck, who is vice-president of the Chamber of Commerce, and Colonel George Pickett, a distinguished citizen of our state, formerly of the U.S. Corps of Engineers and Department of Natural Resources and Community Development, Water Resources.

I will be brief, Mr. Chairman. This project promises to be a source of dependable and sufficient water supply for the city of Raleigh. . . .

The citizens of Raleigh obviously don't have to worry about keeping clean. With the water from Falls Creek and the soft soap from Senator Helms, all they're going to have to supply is the tub.

It may appear at this point as though I have been accusing members of Congress, lobbyists, and agency personnel of the odious crime of friendship. I must hasten to point out that this has not been my intention. Friendship is not a subversive activity, and no one is going to insist that Senator Helms cut Mr. Carper off his Christmas-card list because Mr. Carper is actively lobbying Congress for Falls Creek Lake. The problem is not the friendships themselves. The problem is what the friendships do. They tend to become blinders.

There in that committee room, locked in the soft warm glow of friendly banter and good-old-boy camaraderie, the congressmen have a strong tendency to forget that there are other people. Because his friends want to see Falls Creek Dam built, it is easy for Senator Helms to overlook the fact that there are numerous others in the world, in the nation, in North Carolina, and even in Raleigh who don't want it built. Project opponents, because they are not a part of the circle, become nonpersons. The Iron Triangle looks inward; its members have an extraordinarily strong tendency to listen to no counsel but each other's. And that is a serious flaw. Not just because the counsel is sometimes wrong but because, with no outside standards to measure it, there is no way to tell that it might be wrong. Around and around that triangle the opinions go, reinforcing each other, sloughing off opposing opinions as "nonprofessional" or "politically naive" or as belonging to a few "kooks" who want to "halt progress," and entirely ignoring the possibility that those nonprofessional, politically naive kooks might be expert, dedicated, broadly supported—and right.

This raises what may be the ultimate question about pork barreling. *Does it work?* Do the beneficiaries actually benefit? Do the secondary beneficiaries get their spinoff profits? Most importantly of all, do the congressmen get reelected?

The members of the Iron Triangle are generally not interested in this question, mostly because they think they already know the answer. However, as the taxpayers who are footing the bill, the rest of us cannot afford to be so complacent. It is time to take a closer look at some of these pork-barrel projects and at some of their more glaring design, engineering, and functional failures, and try to discover just what it is that we are footing the bill for.

6
The Pork That Failed

On October 4, 1962, Senator Robert S. Kerr of Oklahoma, known to friends and enemies alike as Big Bob, stood on the floor of the United States Senate and, as chairman of the Public Works Committee, bitterly assailed Senator Caleb Boggs of Delaware for daring to question the decisions of the Army Corps of Engineers. "I wonder if the senator from Delaware knows," Big Bob emphasized, "that most of the assignments to the Corps of Engineers are made from the top ten percent of the graduating class each year at West Point. If there is a highly trained, competent group of engineers in the United States . . . they are to be found in the Corps of Army Engineers.

"The project which the senator from Delaware seeks to strike from this bill was evaluated by the Corps of Engineers, the Board of Rivers and Harbors, the Chief of Engineers, and then by the director of the Bureau of the Budget of the U.S. Government. All of them said that it was economically feasible. Under that circumstance it would be a little presumptuous of me to say it was not economically feasible."

Sixteen years later, in 1978, Senator John Stennis of Mississippi, occupying the same chair that Bob Kerr had filled so flamboyantly in decades past, sat in a Senate hearing room and made much the same sort of remark. "I want to mention here," said Stennis, "the tremendous work of the U.S. Army Corps of Engineers—there are other agencies of the government that do fine work, but none better than the Army Corps. . . . It is just about the finest organization that I know anything about in the entire federal government."

This is Iron Triangle rhetoric, of course. How accurate is it? Is the Corps really the highly elite, superprofessional, stainless-steel body of engineering expertise that men like Kerr and Stennis would have us believe?

The answer, of course, is no. The Corps is human; perhaps no worse than the average engineering firm, but certainly no better. It makes mistakes, and some of those mistakes are lulus. On the Jackson River in Virginia, for example, the Corps' recently completed Gathright Dam had to be redesigned in midriver when the anchor point on one end of the damsite was found to be cavernous limestone, structurally too weak to support the dam. The redesign doubled the dam's cost. On the Missouri River, the back end of the Fort Peck Dam gave way as the reservoir was being filled, killing eight workers. At wide, shallow Carlyle Reservoir in Illinois, the Corps failed to take into account the strong prevailing westerly winds in the area and the wave force that they might be able to kick up on the reservoir's surface. As a result, much of the eastern bank, including some very expensive, taxpayer-constructed picnic facilities, has eroded away. At the Marmes Rockshelter National Historic Site in Washington, the reason for the historic site designation—the rockshelter itself, where among the oldest known human skeletal fragments in North America had been discovered—was drowned by a leaking Corps cofferdam. The list could probably be extended indefinitely.

These are all examples of direct engineering incompetence, of cases where the Corps' projects have failed because of basic structural flaws. But there is also the matter of design incompetence, or failure of the projects to perform as promised. This is also widespread. We have been talking throughout this book of the problems caused by concentrating the beneficiaries of government spending in the districts of a few powerful congressmen or senators, but a close look at the record indicates that even these so-called beneficiaries often do not benefit. At Carlyle Dam (where the recreation facilities are falling into the reservoir), downstream farmers have complained that instead of giving them protection from what used to be brief, disastrous winter floods the dam has given them a water-table rise that has kept their fields flooded for many months at a time. "Instead of flood control, all we got was controlled flooding," complained one "beneficiary" bitterly. The same problem has occurred at Libby Dam in Montana.

Along the Mississippi River, Corps "flood-control" devices and other river manipulations have actually increased flood heights. The 1973 flood, for example, carried only as much water as a typical thirty-year "flood event" on the Mississippi but recorded the highest river levels ever seen at St. Louis. And on the Kissimmee River in Florida, where the Corps channeled the entire river in an attempt to reduce flooding in downstream Lake Okeechobee, the new "Kissimmee Sewer" has performed so badly that river flows which used to be seen only during hurricanes are now routinely observed during moderate rainstorms. The state of Florida has asked the Corps to put the river back the way it was before they began fooling around with it, which will mean an additional cost to the taxpayers of some $50 million.

The Corps' economics are no better than their engineer-

ing. In order to justify projects which they want to build—
or which powerful congressmen want to have built—the
fix-it shop manages to come up with some extremely fasci-
nating pieces of economic reasoning. Nearly all Corps projects, for instance, are justified by amortizing construction
costs at the absolutely astounding interest rate of—hold on
to your hats, folks—3¼ percent. (To be perfectly fair, we
must admit that this is not entirely the Corps' fault. That
interest rate is mandated by Congress, which knows precisely what would happen to its pet projects if they had to
be justified using the current cost of money.) Flood-control
benefits are often computed on the basis of prevention of
damage to future flood-plain development; that is, to buildings that aren't there yet and which probably never will be
if the dam isn't built.

Navigation benefits for barge canals are computed by
using the so-called prevailing rate method (rail rates minus
barge rates times expected tonnage to be carried). This
looks reasonable until you realize that the barge rates are
government subsidized by the canals themselves, which are
built and maintained essentially free of charge to the barge
operators, whereas the rail rates include the cost of con-
structing and keeping up the right-of-way. One Arthur D.
Little study in the mid-1960s found that benefits to the
public using the prevailing rate method were overstated by
a factor of fourteen. And recreation benefits are also typically overstated, usually simply by ignoring the recreation
benefits which will be removed by a project, which can be
significant. A 1969 Oregon Game Commission/Idaho Fish
and Game Department joint study of the Snake River above
and below the Idaho Power Company's Hells Canyon Dam,
for example, found that use on the free-flowing river below
the dam was more than ten times as intense as that on the
reservoir (322 angler-hours per lineal mile on the river;
only 30 on the reservoir). Corps officials were asked point-
blank shortly afterward if they intended to use the results

of this study in computing recreation benefits for future Oregon projects. The answer was no.

I have been picking on the Corps in the preceding few paragraphs because they are the prototypical pork-barrel agency, and because there is a large body of literature about their failings which has been developed over the past two or three decades by an articulate and increasingly well-qualified group of dam fighters who are trying to protect what is left of America's rivers. I don't want to leave the impression that the Corps is alone in its sins, however. It is not. Other agencies share many of the same failings. It was the Bureau of Reclamation's Teton Dam which burst in 1976, with ensuing major loss to life and property. The Department of Energy is pushing the Solar Power Satellite and synthetic fuels, two high-technology, highly porkable "answers" to the energy crisis which are conceded even by their friends to be at least a decade away from successful operation, if they can ever get operational at all. (By way of contrast, solar power, dismissed as "exotic" by the SPS and synfuels crowd, is workable in many types of applications right now. But it also is highly unporkable, at least as long as the government can't control the sun. For that reason it is getting extremely short shrift in federal budget planning.)

Finally, it is the military which wants to build the MX missile, with its multibillion-dollar electric-train setup in the Nevada desert. The proposed track network would be fully one-fourth as long as the entire interstate freeway system. Conservative columnist James J. Kilpatrick calls the project "goofy" and Pentagon watcher Tom Dine at the Brookings Institution charges it cannot possibly be made operational. However, it's obvious that the Defense Department and their friends in the military-contracting business plan to have an awful lot of fun trying.

There *are* public-works projects, military projects, energy grants, and other government expenditures of a locally directed nature that are worthwhile, but sometimes it seems infernally difficult to discover them—not because the bad ones so outnumber the good ones, but because the Iron Triangle refuses to admit that the bad ones exist at all, and will not set up realistic criteria for sorting them out.

So far I have pointed to examples of pork-barrel projects failing to do what they were designed to do: that is, failing to benefit the primary beneficiaries. What about the secondary beneficiaries? Do indirect benefits really accrue to a local economy from having a government project in its midst? Does it really contribute to an area's economic prosperity to have a dam, a missile plant, a canal, or a military base nearby? Do the small businessmen who lobby so desperately for these things get their money's worth out of their lobbying costs?

George Pring doesn't think so. "I find this ironic," he says in his Denver office, "but when a major public-works project goes in, the secondary beneficiaries generally get screwed to the wall. Either the project does not generate the secondary revenues that they thought would occur, or, in the case of all those Ma and Pa outfits, if the project is a real generator of new economy the majors are going to move in and take over. It will no longer be a Ma and Pa store, it will be a Seven-Eleven or a Safeway. It will no longer be a local service station, it'll be bought up as one of the company-owned stations. And one of those two cycles occurs over and over again."

Pring's picture is not pretty, but it is substantially correct. There is a growing body of evidence which suggests that massive public-works projects not only fail to contribute to the local economy but may even become a burden on it. Economist Charles B. Garrison of the University of Tennessee studied secondary benefits arising from Norris Reservoir, the Tennessee Valley Authority's oldest and most popular recreation site. He concluded that ". . . the contribution of recreation expenditures to the local economy has been relatively unimportant. . . . The net result of the income and employment changes occurring in the area was continued out-migration and a small population decrease from 1960 to 1970."

John F. Ballard of the University of Missouri Extension Service studied two Corps of Engineers reservoirs in Illinois and concluded that their presence had *reduced* the tax base in the counties in which they were constructed, leading to economic decline. In west-central Alabama, rural Greene County is bounded on two of its three sides by barge canals. This has not kept it from being ranked among the twenty poorest counties in the United States. In Oregon, sociologists from Oregon State University did a before-and-after study of the city of Sweet Home in relation to the construction of nearby Green Peter Reservoir and concluded that the city had suffered an increased tax load with little or no increase in income—a net loss. ". . . the permanent residents of Sweet Home bore most of the costs of providing school services for children of construction workers who came, stayed a short time, and left," the study group reported in the journal *Rural Sociology*, "and permanent residents also bore the burden of increased indebtedness for expanded municipal services. The expectations by some that postconstruction economic growth would help with these costs did not materialize."

These examples have all been from the water-projects field, but the same could be said of other types of public works. Gordon Adams of the Council on Economic Priorities tackled the secondary benefits of the military pork barrel and concluded, in a 1979 article prepared for the *Christian Science Monitor* news service, that "Ultimately, defense spending contributes to unemployment . . . by sucking resources out of other sectors of the economy and feeding an industry that creates fewer jobs." The public-works program of the Economic Development Administration, designed specifically to capitalize on the secondary-benefici-ary "multiplier effect" by pouring money into economically depressed areas, has been a flat failure. Of 424 such areas targeted for EDA assistance in 1966, 311—nearly 75 per-cent—had seen little or no change in their depressed status a decade later. And as for freeways, those great contribu-tions to the American dream, the San Francisco planning department in 1967 took a look at what the extra traffic they brought in was costing the city and concluded that ". . . each additional automobile entering the downtown [area] during the rush hour requires an additional investment in street and parking space amounting to $25,000." This amount would, of course, have to come out of municipal revenues. At that rate, any economic benefits coming into the area because of the new freeway would almost certainly be more than offset by higher taxes. "You wish," sighs Pring, "that there was some way you could tell the second-ary beneficiaries in advance, 'Look, here's what's going to happen to you. You're not going to reap the benefits of this in any fashion—in fact, it may put you out of business.' But that's hard to sell."

Hard, indeed. But hard as it is to sell the secondary beneficiaries on the idea that they may not benefit from a project, or that they may actually suffer a net loss, there is another group of people who are even more resistant to buying this idea. These people absolutely insist that the pork-barrel projects they are pushing so hard *are* doing a job for them, and they clearly do not want to listen to any evidence to the contrary. The job is ensuring reelection. The group is Congress itself.

There was once—and still is, in some minds—a grand Corps of Engineers–barge lobby–land developer scheme to spend $2 billion of your hard-earned tax dollars to turn the Dallas–Fort Worth area in central Texas into a seaport. The mechanics were simple, straightforward, and utterly preposterous. All they had to do, it developed, was to turn six hundred miles of the meandering, tree-lined Trinity River into a straight, riprap-lined ditch, add a couple of giant reservoirs to provide the water to flush boats through the necessary locks, and presto! Ocean-going vessels in downtown Dallas. Never mind that the U.S. Fish and Wildlife Service had computed probable dollar loss to the Gulf of Mexico commercial fishery from the project at $1.7 million, or that the river's lower hundred miles had been identified by conservationists, the Texas Division of Parks and Wildlife, and even by the Corps itself as an area of "outstanding wilderness and scenic characteristics." Never mind that the project wasn't even needed: Dallas is served by four perfectly good rail lines, and at least one chamber of commerce spokesman admitted at the height of local passion for the project that he "didn't think not having a canal would hurt the Dallas economy at all." There is something romantic about the image of great vessels loading up at a city's wharves, even if the great vessels are only going to be barge trains. Let 'er rip!

Any time you let 'er rip, of course, there's somebody up there doing the ripping. In Dallas's case, this function was served by something called the Trinity Improvement Association, which *Texas Observer* contributing editor Dan Gardner charges was "organized and run by the Dallas–Fort Worth plutocracy and largely funded by the utility companies." True to the concept of the Iron Triangle, the Corps of Engineers worked closely with the TIA from the organization's beginnings in the 1930s, but it was not until 1955 that things really got cozy. In that year, the association managed to convince the state government to incorporate a quasi-official agency called the Trinity River Authority, which was just the TIA under a different set of hats. The boards of directors of the two organizations were virtually interchangeable for many years, and at one time a single individual, Ben Carpenter, served as chairman of both bodies. The Corps has a standing congressional mandate to cooperate with state agencies, and the Trinity River Authority clearly qualified. Coordination of planning between the two was soon almost obscene. Texas politicians, convinced by the Corps and by the TRA/TIA members that they were dealing with constituency desires, quickly hopped on the bandwagon. The Trinity Barge Canal was authorized in 1965.

There was only one problem. No one had bothered to ask the constituents if they really wanted TIA's ditch, and suddenly, beginning in the early 1970s, it became quite clear that they didn't.

In the 1972 election, the first of what was to be a series of test votes on the canal question, the voters threw out Representative Earl Cavelle, a genial former mayor of Dallas who ran on a strong procanal platform, and replaced him with a young anticanal Republican named Alan Steelman.

In 1973, the same voters denied, by an almost two-to-one margin, the right of the Trinity River Authority to tax them in order to come up with money for the local share of project costs.

In 1976, voters across the state turned down $400 million in water-development bonds designed to accomplish the same thing. And in 1978, they voted out another procanal congressman, Representative Dale Milford, and replaced him with anticanal candidate Martin Frost.

In early 1980, the Trinity River Barge Canal, once called "the oldest floating crap game in Texas," languishes. "It's on the ropes," says one opponent, "and we intend to keep it there." This particular iron triangle has turned out to be shaky. Somebody took a rivet out of the local interest-group corner, and the whole thing collapsed.

This raises some interesting questions. How many other iron triangles across the country are in a similar state of near collapse? How many federal projects and programs are built on a presumed constituency interest which actually does not exist? How much of the pork barrel is built on misconceptions, and how far afield has the pork ethic been led in supporting them? If Congress ever really looked at pork barreling, ever sat down to examine realistically what the pork barrel has done for it and what sort of a support structure that huge pile of logs they have rolled in over the last couple of centuries has built, what would they find?

Not, it turns out, what they think they would. The truth is that despite all the rhetoric about how their constituents demand these things, despite the pleas by desperate congressmen to their colleagues on the committees that they can't get reelected without something from the barrel to take home and wave around, there is surprisingly little solid evidence to suggest that pork, logrolling, district inviolacy, and all the rest is necessary for congressional survival. In fact, much of what evidence there is points the other way.

The Trinity River Barge Canal story is no anomaly. There are numerous other examples of pork that wasn't wanted by those in whose name it was being sought, and of House and Senate careers built by members of Congress who either ignore the pork ethic or actively oppose it. One thinks immediately of Senators William Proxmire and Gaylord Nelson of Wisconsin, two of the Senate's staunchest pork fighters. They come from a state which consistently ranks at the bottom on all lists of government largesse, and both still get reelected handily every six years. There is also Representative Bob Edgar of Pennsylvania, the greatest water-pork opponent in the House, who has managed to win election and reelection every two years since 1974 despite the fact that he is a Democrat running in a district that has two-thirds Republican voter registration. And there is vehemently and vocally antipork Representative Jim Weaver, who has built his traditionally marginal Oregon Fourth District into what is officially recognized as the safest seat in the Oregon delegation for the 1980 elections, even though that delegation also includes one of the most powerful men in the House, twelve-term veteran Al Ullman, chairman of the House Ways and Means Committee. None of these men appears to have been lowered too far in the esteem of his colleagues by his refusal to roll logs or to suck the crumbs out of the bottom of the pork barrel. Proxmire is chairman of the Senate Banking Committee, Nelson of the Senate's Select Committee on Small Business. Edgar chairs the 213-member Northeast-Midwest Caucus in the House, and Weaver not only chairs the important Forestry Subcommittee of the House Agriculture Committee—a position he broke precedent by vaulting into after only one term—but was also hand-picked by his colleagues to head the House investigation into 1979's Three Mile Island nuclear plant near-disaster.

Losses? There have been a few. Proxmire's failure to win his forest-products laboratory for Madison, Wisconsin, is one conspicuous example. But on the whole these losses have not been very noticeable. Asked to name some pet projects that have been denied to the people of Pennsylvania's Seventh District as a result of Bob Edgar's almost rabid antipork stance, Edgar aide Sallie Phillips says with a mild shrug that she "can't think of anything." And Weaver makes much the same point, though in somewhat more picturesque terms. "When I got back here, you know," he told me in his Washington office, "I'd have some Texas chairman sit down next to me in the House, and he'd say, 'Now look here, boy. You vote for oil, or we won't give you any of your projects out there.' Well, it turns out, half the projects in my district I didn't want anyway. So they were no threat to me. And the interesting thing is that they threatened me again and again—you know, if I didn't vote for them on this, if I didn't vote for them on that, they'd cut off something. And I didn't vote with them. On the contrary, I led the fights against them—and they've never cut off a single project in my district. I guess the Corps wants 'em, or *somebody* wants 'em, because they just keep going on."

The experiences of Weaver, Edgar, Proxmire, and Nelson indicate strongly that pork is not a necessary component of political success. The experiences of others go further. There are numerous examples of cases where pork actually has damaged political careers, at least in the eyes of the electorate, where it really counts. Old Joe Martin of Massachusetts, who served either as House minority leader or as Speaker in every Congress from 1939 until his defeat in 1966 at the ripe age of eighty-two, used to delight in telling the tale of his near-disastrous encounter with pork during his freshman term in the House in 1925. "When I was first elected to Congress," he wrote in his autobiography, *My First Fifty Years in Politics*, ". . . I fell heir to the old Taunton River issue. For a hundred years my district had been interested in having the river widened and deepened to make it navigable for steamers.

"Where my predecessors failed I got the necessary legislation through Congress, only to find it the biggest issue raised against me in the next election. The railroads were angry because it threatened them with new competition. The gas company people were furious because they feared that they would be put to great expense removing their pipes from the river bed. The owners of a large stove company at Taunton were frantic lest the widening of the river weaken the foundation of their factory. And to top it off many of the voters were suspicious that I, who was to become a veritable symbol of economy in government, was a big spender."

Others could repeat similar tales of woe. For example, Jennings Randolph of West Virginia, a power in the Senate since 1958, came within a hair's breadth of defeat in the 1978 election. Common wisdom says that Randolph's narrow escape was due to his advancing age, but this may not be so. "Randolph said the day before the election that he expected to win by 75,000 votes," one of his constituents told me as she trudged around Washington seeking votes against one of Randolph's pet pork barrels, the Stonewall Jackson Dam. "He did win, but it was only by 4,000 votes. And in our county, at least, the dam was not just *an* issue. It was *the* issue." The same election saw the defeat of Representative Dale Milford of Texas by Democrat Martin Frost in the primary, at least partially over the issue of the Trinity River Barge Canal which Milford ardently backed and Frost (and the majority of Texas voters) opposed. It also saw the downfall of Representative John McFall of California, whom the League of Conservation Voters once characterized as the "king of pork-barrel water politics in California," by Republican challenger Norman Shumway in a campaign in which McFall's strident and unbending support of the New Melones Dam was one of the principal issues.

Veteran pork fighters have numerous stories of this nature. One of Brent Blackwelder's favorites concerns the Oakley Dam in Illinois, which was defeated, he claims, "simply by embarrassing the member so often that he retired. It was just too much trouble to be a member. They created too much pressure in the district, the guy was having to leave his parties in Washington to go back to the district all the time, and whenever he'd be back there, a group of farmers would be bugging him about why they'd be losing their land to this boondoggle. It got to be too much for him, and the project was stopped." Over at Common Cause, Bruce Adams remarks that the tide on pork seems to be turning: "I would argue that one thing that we have going for us here is that there is probably a growing perception by the younger members of Congress that pork *can* hurt—that there are forces at work which can make it seem less attractive to just pile all these things up, as in the past." Blackwelder agrees, quoting a piece of advice he attributes to Senator Herman Talmadge of Georgia:

"Never be at the ceremony for a dam, because the people in the area that you have taken never forgive you for what you've done."

But if all this is true, why is pork still so powerful? If antipork congressmen have little trouble remaining in Congress and advancing in the political power structure, and if those who wallow in the pork lard are often defeated, either in spite of this wallowing or because of it, why does it remain business as usual down at the Great Washington Pork Factory? Why does the pork keep pouring forth in such dizzying, unending streams?

Part of the problem may simply be that not enough congressmen have yet grasped the points made by Adams and Blackwelder. Too many still see the barrel as the easy way to votes, whether it is or not. George Pring: "I think that the answer to that is that it is *perceived* to be so, therefore it *is* so. In other words, as long as the Congress member sees that he derives votes from implementing projects in his district, it will become a self-fulfilling prophecy. People will perceive that he feels that way, and therefore be pressured to get out the vote for him, otherwise they won't get the projects. It's a nice little circle. It may be totally wrong, but as long as both sides believe that the other side believes it, they're locked into the pattern."

Besides, Pring argues, even if a congressman suspects that the pork barrel is sinking, he is not going to abandon it unless he can be convinced that something more buoyant is floating along on the political tide that he can latch onto. "Nobody in this day and age," he points out, "really wants to be caught urging taxpayer expenditures, particularly on those projects that can be ridiculed on the basis of million-dollars-per-farm logic. So we may be seeing some real changes. We've certainly heard a lot of rhetoric that way, and it may become an effective argument. But if so, you're going to have to show the congressperson how he can get

votes by some *other* sure fashion. Because despite Proposi-
tion 13, the antitax concept has just not become a reliable
voter constituency." Everyone wants to cut taxes, but the
minute you make a serious attempt to do so you're faced
with a million conflicting ideas about where those cuts
should take place, and a million conflicting ideas simply
cannot form a single constituency. You go back to "I want
to cut federal spending, and by the way, our local hospital
needs work." Those who want pork may clearly be a minority, but they are an organized minority, and one knows
where one stands with them. One hesitates to abandon
them without an equally reliable group to take their place.

And even if such a group were found, there would remain a serious problem. Even if a congressman can be
shown a vigorous and coherent antipork constituency
within his district, even if he can see the Edgars and the
Proxmires advancing in the House and Senate despite their
vehement antipork stands, even if he knows that the barrel
is just as adept at running over its supporters as its opponents, he may still remain loyal to it. He may still vote for
others' pork projects and push his own with a single-
minded and terrible intensity. The problem is not that he
is a fool, or contrary, or blind. The problem is simply that
he is a human being, with humanly fixed opinions and
humanly staunch resistance to acting against the dictates of
his own conscience. He doesn't need a million dollars from
a lobbyist to convince him to vote for a dam if he already
believes in the dam. He doesn't need a thousand Lockheed
employees breathing down his neck to convince him to
work hard for a military contract if Lockheed is his neigh-
bor and Boeing, Douglas, Martin-Marietta, and General
Dynamics are not. We all prefer what we know to what we
don't know. We all trust our own beliefs much further than
we trust the beliefs of others. Congressmen are no different.

"The people who are on the committees," says Joel

Aberbach of the Brookings Institution with typical preci-
sion, "are interested in getting projects done. It's within
the context of their world view. The assumption is that
these public-works projects are a good idea, and within that
context they're interested primarily in seeing that these
projects serve the needs of the people who want them."

Jim Weaver agrees. "Pork barrel," he emphasizes, "is not
just the constituency. Pork barrel is a pattern of mind. The
committees are dominated by the people who like to build
things like nuclear plants and dams, and so they build them,
even though they're having trouble now finding places to
put them, even if a member doesn't want them in his district.

"You know, in the old days, in the New Deal, a dam was
the hope. It was! The dam sites then were worth something. You could produce power and some other things,
and there was the hope of jobs. Now these people, these old
pork-barreling congressmen, their minds were made up in
the thirties when people were desperate, you've got to remember that. And so they're *still* for that dam, even if it's
absolutely valueless. The fact that it's valueless just doesn't
matter."

But if Weaver and Aberbach are right—and I think they
are—where do we go from here? If pork is a world view and
a pattern of mind, how do we shift to another view and
another pattern? If dams were the hope in the thirties,
where is the hope today? Is there any hope?

I think that there is, and strangely enough, I think the
spot to look for it is within the pork ethic itself. Because
despite all the damage it has done, despite all the unneeded
dams it has built, the outmoded military bases it has preserved, and all the other things, the pork ethic is basically
a positive value. Congressmen want to do things for the
people who elect them. That is the gist of it. Most congressmen are development-minded, and so they roll out the
pork barrel every year to accomplish this. But it doesn't

have to be that way at all. The task of the pork-barrel reformer is really very simple: to find some way to show our congressmen that they have developed enough, and that what the people who elect them really want is for them to nail the lid on that barrel and roll it back.

In the next—and final—chapter, we'll cover a few of the ways in which this might be done.

7

Living Low on the Hog

This is the story of a pork-barrel reform that failed, on our way to an explanation of a couple that might succeed.

The story begins on February 22, 1977, just one month after Jimmy and Rosalynn Carter's triumphal hand-in-hand walk down Pennsylvania Avenue on Inauguration Day. One of the principal planks in Carter's election platform had been a pledge to attack the pork barrel, and he was losing no time in doing it. Before the ink was dry on the election results, Carter had a team of economic advisors going over Gerald Ford's lame-duck presidential budget. Now in late February, using his prerogatives under the Budget Act, the new president was ready to move. In his message to Congress concerning recommended changes in the Ford budget, he announced that he would seek to terminate funding for nineteen massive pork-barrel water projects which his advisors considered "environmentally or economically unsound or potentially hazardous," and that others were being reviewed to see if they might warrent similar action.

Congress's reaction to this sledgehammer attack on its pork prerogatives was swift. The very next day, February

23, Interior Secretary Cecil Andrus found himself sum-
moned before the House Interior Committee and given a
blunt warning: Lay off! Emerging from the meeting, the
secretary was collared by reporters. What had transpired?
Andrus grinned wanly. "The message I got," he said, "was
that if a member had a water project, he didn't want it
cancelled." No news there, of course. The president would
fight on.

On March 10, an even stronger message came down
from the Senate. Before passing an urgently needed emer-
gency appropriations measure, the senators added a rider
prohibiting the president from cutting funds for those
nineteen disputed projects. "The road can be smooth or
the road can be rough," warned Senate Majority Leader
Robert Byrd, throwing down a very obvious gauntlet.
Carter's attack on pork, he said, had "rubbed a raw nerve"
in the Senate. If the president wanted a confrontation, he
was certainly going about it the right way. What did he say
to that?

Carter's answer was conciliatory in tone but not in content. "I am aware of your concerns and I sympathize with
them," he wrote in an open letter to Congress, "but I
cannot meet my commitment to balance the budget unless
the Congress and I can cooperate in reducing unnecessary
spending." If Congress were sincere about wanting to
bring inflation under control, they were going to have to
help.

The next several months resembled an arm-wrestling
contest with a barrel of salt pork as the table. The list of
axed projects, now known as the "hit list," grew to thirty,
then shrank again to a final count of eighteen. The House
passed its version of the annual Public Works Appropriations bill, funding all but one of the hit-list projects and
adding twelve new ones. A fuming Carter threatened a
veto. House Majority Leader Tip O'Neill, dining at the
White House, told the president bluntly that the veto could

not possibly stick. The Senate version came out of committee with the hit list precisely halved, nine projects eliminated and nine funded. The president announced that in
the spirit of compromise he would accept the Senate version. The House concurred, and on August 8 the bill was
signed into law. Score: Congress 9, Carter 9. The first
round had ended in a draw.

The second round would be all Carter's.

The first of what would turn out to be two major confron-
tations in this second round began on September 27, 1978,
with passage by the Senate of the conference report on the
Public Works Appropriations Bill for Fiscal Year 1979, the
same vehicle on which the compromise over the hit list had
been reached the year before. The bill, which had clearly
gone through the congressional pork wallow on a business-
as-usual basis, had funding for fifty-three projects. The
president was stunned: He had asked for twenty-six.
Worse, the bill contained funds for six of the nine projects
which the hit-list compromise had supposedly killed the
year before, added 2,300 new bureaucrats to the Corps of
Engineers' civilian staff at a time when the administration
had taken a firm stand in favor of cutting down the bureaucracy, and eliminated funding for the Water Resources
Council, an agency which Carter was depending heavily
upon to formulate a set of new water-policy standards with
which pork fighters could attack the worst of the water-pork
projects.

Calling the bill "wasteful," "inflationary," and "absolutely unacceptable," Carter pledged a veto in fervent if
slightly ungrammatical terms: "I, along with the people of
our country, are tired of seeing taxpayers' money wasted."
That was on October 3. On October 5 the veto came, along
with a full-page ad in the *Washington Post* bought and paid
for by Howard Jarvis, the mastermind of California's Prop-
osition 13. The ad attacked the bill as "an outrage!" and
proclaimed that "any politician who supports this bill now

must have his head in the sand." That message, plus some intense personal lobbying by the president himself, got through. The veto was sustained 190–223, 53 votes short of the two-thirds needed to override.

Well! Shock waves rippled through the pork lard. The last president with the guts to veto a public-works bill had been Dwight Eisenhower, and his veto had been overridden. But if the demise of the appropriations bill was a shock, there was an even bigger thunderstroke awaiting the pork barrel less than a month away: the defeat, through some very adroit footwork on the part of antipork legislators and lobbyists, of the Omnibus Rivers and Harbors Authorization Bill of 1978, the Public Works Committees' vehicle by which future pork projects would be prepared for appropriations. In this case, $4 billion worth of future projects went sloshing merrily down the drain. It was a genuine double whammy. Not only would there be no money for pork this year, but next year there might not even be a place to put the money. Score: Carter 121, Congress 0—121 projects killed and none passed.

Pork fighters, of course, were overjoyed. They saw it as a smashing blow against the whole cozy, back-scratching system. Some were still seeing it that way as much as eight months later. "This administration has had an effective role on water projects," Presidential Assistant Jim Free told me happily at the White House in June. "Because of sustaining that veto, Congress knows the White House has the power to veto, and it's going to make them more cautious." In fact, Free said, Jimmy Carter's only regret was that he hadn't vetoed the hit-list compromise of the year before. "The president has admitted that the biggest mistake of his first year was being too conciliatory." Brave words, certainly, but not without reason to be so. The field appeared to be won.

Why, then, was it so shortly afterwards that the victorious army was in disarray, banners streaming backwards, bugles blowing retreat? Why, on September 25, less than a hundred days after Free and I spoke, did President Carter sign into law one of the worst pork-barrel bills of all time, the $10.6-billion Energy and Water Development Act of 1979? Among other things, this act called for construction starts on nine projects which were outside both the presidential and congressional budgets and on which the Corps of Engineers had not completed either economic or environmental review; for the acceleration of funding schedules for a number of controversial projects in an attempt to ram them through before the controversy could be settled; for the starving to death once more of the Water Resources Council by failing to provide any operating funds with which to monitor Corps and Bureau of Reclamation projects; and, worst of all, for a waiver of the Endangered Species Act and "all other laws" so that the Tennessee Valley Authority could complete the highly controversial Tellico Dam.

This last undoubtedly grieved pork fighters the most. Though the press had played up Tellico as nothing much more than a case of Senator Howard Baker of Tennessee vs. a three-inch fish (the now-famous endangered snail darter), Tellico was actually one of the biggest boondoggles of all time. It was a $100-million taxpayer ripoff that violated at least five federal statutes besides the Endangered Species Act and had been rejected by a blue-ribbon panel of presidential economic advisors fewer than nine months before on purely dollars-and-cents grounds (the panel found that the dam's annual benefits would be $700,000 less than its annual maintainance costs, and that it would be more cost-effective to tear down the nearly complete structure than to finish it). Primarily, critics charged, it was a "speculative real-estate enterprise by the Tennessee Valley Authority." Speculative real-estate enterprises clearly do not fall within the purview of either Congress or the Tennessee Valley Authority, but there it was. The much-heralded pork-barrel reforms of 1978 lay broken, the shards of them scattered thickly about the valley of the Little Tennessee River. Why? What went wrong?

Part of the reason, surely, can be traced to sheer, raw, unadulterated politics on the part of the House of Representatives, which saw in the Tellico issue a test of the district-inviolacy principle and the ability of a representative to get what he wants out of the government for the people of his district. The House had given notice in a number of not-so-subtle ways that Tellico was nonnegotiable. The Tellico exemption broke a long-standing House rule against making policy on appropriations bills, and the leadership had snuck it through for the first time on a parliamentary move of questionable legality (the amendment was never read on the floor and the few House members present had no idea what they were voting for, other than that the committee leadership approved of it). But once in place, it proved to have all the fiendish tenacity of used bubble gum. The Senate rejected it three times; the House put it back. Sending the bill over to the White House for Carter's signature, House Majority Leader Wright told the president that if he vetoed, "it would just add fuel to the fire, and he probably wouldn't get anything else out of Congress." Then, just to make sure, the House began to attach identical Tellico riders to virtually every bill it passed. Though the president was accused by environmental leaders of giving in to the pork interests ("He had a chance to show leadership," moaned Brent Blackwelder to the press, "and he blew it"), sober consideration indicates that he really had very little choice. It was hello Tellico or good-bye Congress.

And that brings us to the real reason the president's valiant pork-reform efforts failed. It was not that they were ineffective or poorly enforced; it was not that Congress had run roughshod over them, nor that a weak president had given in, nor that the special interests had gutted them. It was much deeper than that. The reforms failed not because of any internal flaw, but because they were reforms of the wrong things.

Jimmy Carter had tackled water-project standards, but the pork barrel knows no standards. He had tried to reform the cost-benefit ratio, but he had forgotten the Corps' fix-it shop. He had written new rules of the game, but it wasn't his game. Congress owned the cards, and Congress didn't need to follow Jimmy's rules. If it didn't like the way the game was going, Congress could pick up the chips and go home.

"The Carter administration is making a valuable attempt to establish some criteria," Bruce Adams of Common Cause told me well before the veto was announced. "The problem, though, is that Congress has not disciplined itself to stick to the criteria it's got, even though those criteria aren't very good. I think that's the long and short of it. To the extent that you make it more public, and get serious about your analysis, you have a basis on which members of Congress who want to stand up against the system—which is a hard thing to do—have a better opportunity to do it. So raising visibility and improving analysis and establishing criteria are ways to set up a counter system against the good-old-boy pork-barrel network, and those would be the kind of things that we at Common Cause would be for. But that's not the total answer. Because it's really a matter of the institution of Congress itself, and its visibility and its discipline. And it has a lot more visibility now than it used to have, but it seems to have less discipline. And I think all these criteria can help you hold to discipline. But ultimately, at least in the case of these water projects, they don't seem to do it very well."

For every Tellico Dam there is an Endangered Species Act exemption. For every Alaska Pipeline there is a National Environmental Policy Act exemption. For every failure of benefit/cost analysis, there is a repair part in the agency's fix-it shop. Standards are meaningless unless they are adhered to, and there is nothing short of the Constitution itself that can force Congress to adhere to anything.

But if not standards, what? If no one but Congress can impose discipline and Congress will not do so, whence then the discipline? Has this whole book been merely whistling in the dark?

Perhaps. And perhaps not. Let's take a look at some of the things that are being done, along with attempts to tighten standards and improve criteria, at various public-interest lobby organizations around Washington.

At Common Cause and at Ralph Nader's Congress Watch, hopes are pinned on campaign-financing reform. The theory behind this is simple and straightforward. If special-interest groups, including district interests, are prohibited from giving massive campaign contributions to congressmen, they will have no more influence over those congressmen than the rest of us do. The congressmen will thus be free to consider larger issues more openly. Currently, congressmen too often look at their list of contributors to find out who their friends are. "Special-interest money pouring into political campaigns," write two Common Cause staffers, Jan Cook and Nancy Gager, in the organization's 1979 study *How Money Talks in Congress,* "is contributing to legislative paralysis and interest-group domination of Congress. . . . While substantial campaign contributions may not actually 'buy' votes, they do ensure easy access to public officials and create an unhealthy atmosphere of familiarity." They quote Senator Russell Long and business executive Justin Dart. Political contributions are "bread cast upon the waters to be returned a thousand-fold" (Long); dialogue with politicans "is a fine thing but with a little money they hear you better" (Dart). Are they correct?

Perhaps so. There is little doubt that the candidate who spends the most is likely to win the election (studies have shown that repeatedly), and that once in, that candidate is likely to feel beholden to those who made winning possible. There is also the small but significant point that the special interests are not likely to give any money to a candidate unless he or she is already sympathetic to their goals. As Edward Maher of the National Association of Manufacturers once observed, "If you get the right group down there, you don't have to lobby." In 1968, 90 percent of the campaign contributions for Representative Edward A. Garnatz of Maryland, at that time the chairman of the House Merchant Marine and Fisheries Committee, came from maritime interests with issues before the committee. When confronted with this fact, Garnatz was indignant—not with the contributions, but with the fact that anyone should question them. "Who the hell did they expect me to get it from," he snapped, "the Post Office?" Who indeed—someone who didn't like Garnatz's proshipping industry votes? Of course not. People contribute to the campaign of the candidate they agree with, and they make the contribution because they are convinced that when the candidate gets into office he will vote the "right" way. Finding some way to guarantee equal spending by both sides in every congressional election would reduce the ability of special interests to get their pocket candidates elected, and that would certainly cut into the effectiveness of the pork barrel. The idea has merit.

Unfortunately, it also has its drawbacks. For one thing, it would be horrendously expensive. Devoting just $50,000 in public funds to each congressional and senatorial final election—a very minimal figure these days—would cost the federal treasury $25 million every two years. It would be difficult to police—who would rule as to what was a campaign expense and what was not? And though it would certainly cut the power of the nationally oriented special interests, the district-oriented ones wouldn't suffer very much. The congressman would still be bound by the pork

ethic, still committed to doing special things for his constituents without regard to what they might do to the country as a whole. I suspect that campaign-finance reform is
both necessary and desirable, but I don't expect it to solve
the pork problem all by itself. We must look elsewhere.

What about the balanced-budget amendment? That's
the approach they're pushing over at the National Taxpayers' Union. Again, the basic reasoning behind it is quite
sound. The federal budget is currently put together incre-
mentally, with the holistic approach provided by the House
and Senate Budget Committees mere window-dressing
with no real power. Placing an upper limit on federal
spending, the theory goes, would force a serious holistic
look at the budget, a merciless scrutinizing for waste as the
fiscal planners look for places to cut to get the total under
the limit. It would become that much harder to justify
purely pork-barrel projects.

"You have to have *some* kind of limit to spending, either
to what they can take in through taxes—sort of a mechani-
cal limit—or to a figure decided by a vote of the people,"
NTU's David Keating argues. "What you have now, basically, is all these spending things being lumped together.
If people could take a vote on the total spending figure, or
on the taxes that support it, there's no doubt they'd vote
it down. But when you add spending up through the present system of everybody running in for a piece of it, you'll
get a significantly higher figure. That's why you see this
movement for some sort of constitutional limit on the budget. People just figure there's no way you're ever going to
counteract these spending interests, and this logrolling and
pork-barreling, without some limit." The criteria that
Bruce Adams complains "Congress has not disciplined itself to stick to" would *have* to be stuck to, or the limit
couldn't be met.

Like campaign-finance reform, the balanced-budget idea
is an almost irresistibly attractive one, and some form of it

should probably be enacted. But it, too, has its drawbacks. It would reduce flexibility. Though the balanced-budget advocates are fond of pointing to the fact that the United States got by fine with a balanced budget until 1960, they usually fail to point out that this balanced budget was achieved by running deficits in some years and surpluses in others, an approach that would be impossible under a strict balanced-budget approach. Everybody hates deficits, but do we really want to do away with surpluses, too? Should we strait-jacket fiscal planning that tightly?

If we did, what would be strait-jacketed? Would it be the projects and programs that are the most wasteful, or would it be the projects and programs with the least amount of political clout behind them? As long as budgets are made in Congress and Congress is composed of politicians, does anyone doubt what the answer to this question is? "There is," an agency budget official complained not long ago to journalist Leonard Reed, "almost an inverse relationship between the value of a program and the amount of political pressure it generates. The worse a program is, the more likely it has survived because it is somebody's image builder." It won't be the image builders that get cut. It will be the invisible programs that nobody will miss until they're gone. Instead of trimming the waste out of the budget, there is a real risk that the balanced-budget amendment may end up trimming the solid programs and leaving us with a budget that is liberally marbled with pork fat.

There are a number of other attractive ideas floating around, all of them with some merit. One that has been strongly advocated by President Carter is the concept that General Itschner worked so hard to get John Ferejohn's "Senator X" to accept—full funding, or making Congress appropriate all the funds for a project at once instead of spreading it out in yearly increments. Ending credit buying in this manner, the argument goes, would force Congress to take a look at the real cost of some of these turkeys and might contribute to the downfall of those that were the least cost-effective.

Another Carter idea which has received strong support both from antipork workers and from the pork-barreling agencies themselves is that of cost sharing, where local and state governments are required to pay part of the costs of federal projects of primary benefit to a small area. Today, most pork-barrel projects and programs are funded entirely by the federal government, which means that one congressional district may be receiving all of the benefits but paying only 1/434 of the costs (i.e., just 0.2 percent). If the local share of the costs were raised to a more realistic level—say 20 percent—we might see less of a push to build projects or begin programs which were not cost-effective. Current regulations regarding water projects, the army's Don Dillon points out, ordain cost sharing for nonstructural flood-control measures such as flood-plain zoning and flood insurance and for "local protection measures" such as dikes, levees, and channel work, but leave the federal government picking up the entire tab for the big dams. "It has, I think, contributed to a bias toward the structural projects, and has been an obstacle to adopting nonstructural projects," says Dillon. "Nonstructural projects would have had a greater local share of the costs, so they have chosen a structural project, which is maybe not the best one for the site."

"Sunset" legislation, requiring periodic reauthorization of antiquated programs, might help, in that the pork would have to justify itself over and over again, and not just once. So might the practice, pushed by economist Alan Greenspan, of requiring a two-thirds vote to pass all money bills. ("I think the pork barrelers and logrollers would concede that a supermajority vote of that magnitude would be successful in stopping a lot of that," says NTU's David Keating.) Perhaps the most creative is a scheme being pushed by the Environmental Policy Center to use the pork barrel's own techniques against itself, logrolling together an omnibus bill to deauthorize fifteen of the worst pork-barrel water projects. "The idea," says Brent Blackwelder, "is to use the Omnibus Rivers and Harbors approach in reverse, and get so many projects together that people want *off* the list that nobody will dare vote against it." It has proved easy for a congressman to vote for a bill that has waste scattered all through it, but who is going to be able to stand up to his constituents after voting down a bill that is explicitly aimed at curtailing waste? EPC may not get anywhere with this particular bill, but the possibilities look extremely intriguing.

All these approaches appear valuable. Each of them, if adopted, might go a little way toward curbing the power of the pork barrel. If all were adopted, they might go a long way. Unfortunately, however, it appears that none of them, either singly or in any conceivable combination, can go far enough. The reason for this rather gloomy prediction is simple. None of these pork-barrel cures can ultimately be effective because they all contain the same basic flaw: They are attacking the wrong part of the problem. They are going after the pork barrel, and that is good. But the real problem is not the pork barrel; it is the pork ethic.

As long as the pork ethic remains powerful, Congress will find a way to enforce it. As long as each congressman believes that a major part of his duties consists of, in House Majority Leader Wright's words, "producing desirable results for his own district," the pork barrel will roll on. As long as pork remains a desirable commodity, our elected representatives will continue to deal in it. Attacking the pork barrel without attacking the pork ethic is like attacking the symptoms without attacking the disease. It is like making minor adjustments in your tennis game when everybody else is playing ice hockey. And I am deeply afraid that there will be no meaningful reform in the pork-barrel system until this fact is fully grasped by the reformers. They are visualizing a utopian ideal that unfortunately still seems unapproachably remote.

But perhaps I am being too hard on the reformers. The pork ethic, after all, is a tough nut to crack. It may even be impossible to crack. Bang it with a hammer and it just skids sideways across the floor. Bite down on it with restrictive laws, and no matter how powerful the statutory teeth, the only cracks that appear are likely to be those in the laws. The pork ethic is fundamentally and inseparably part of representational democracy, and there is no way to destroy the one without destroying the other. Is what I ask impossible to achieve?

Maybe, but I don't think so. Difficult, yes, but not impossible. There is a key: *It is not necessary to destroy the pork ethic to control it.* We can outflank it instead. In fact, we can use it against itself. Is pork barreling a result of the budget-makers' looking out too tightly for their own constituencies? Very well. Let them continue to do that. *But, somewhere along the line, let us inject into the process a constituency that is all of us.*

That sounds tricky, but it may not be so. I am about to suggest two relatively easy ways to go about it. Neither is new; both have been around for quite a while. Both would require constitutional amendments, but neither amendment would radically alter basic democratic principles. In fact, they might even enhance them. Each has its drawbacks, but none of these drawbacks seems very serious. Most important, each would take away a substantial part of the pork ethic's domination over the federal budget and give it instead, in one form or another, to a national constituency. The ethic itself would not be disturbed; each congressman would still be responsible to his own constituents and would have to "perform creditably" to get himself reelected. But its ability to dictate how and where our taxes should be spent would be vastly reduced. Constituent services would go back to being constituent services, and would stop masquerading as a valid means of making policy and spending decisions that affect all of us.

Of the two methods, the one that is both simpler and more easily operated is that which we shall call the budgetary line-item veto. As the Constitution now stands, the president must either sign or veto the entire text of each bill precisely as Congress gives it to him. He may not pick and choose which portions of the bill appeal to him and which do not, signing some and vetoing others. A budgetary line-item veto would leave that machinery intact for most bills, but would alter it for appropriations bills, allowing the president to single out individual items of appropriation within a large bill and veto them while signing the bulk of the bill into law.

We must be careful here. As a general provision of law, prohibiting line-item vetoes is extremely sound. It assures that Congress and not the president is the primary molder of the nation's laws, and as such gives us a strong insurance policy against the development of a dictatorship. If the president could veto any part of any bill that displeased him, all lawmaking would become subsidiary to one person's whim; democracy would, for all practical purposes, vanish. This is not an area in which tampering should be undertaken lightly.

And yet there remain excellent and convincing reasons to adjust the veto power and thereby modify the relationship it implies between the legislative and executive branches—provided that such modifications can be clearly and carefully limited. The president is, after all, the only elected official in the nation with a truly national constituency, the only individual in government who is responsible to all of us. Each congressman is elected by the voters of a single district, and bears no responsibility to the people on the other side of the mountain; each senator is elected by the voters of a single state. A senator from Colorado could not care less about what the people of New Jersey think of the Fryingpan Dam or of federal subsidies for oil-shale development. What they think is of no consequence to him, because they have no power over his election. To the president, however, all districts are important, all states consequential. He, too, has the pork ethic, but on a grand scale. When he performs creditably for the people of his district he performs creditably for the nation, because his district *is* the nation.

The same forces that work to create waste in Congress work against waste in the presidency. As long as your constituents can keep all the benefits of the projects you bring them but can pawn off the majority of the costs on others, the benefits to them far outweigh the costs to them and they see you as a provider. But as soon as there is no other constituency to share the costs with, total benefits must be measured against total costs—if you advocate projects that are not cost-effective your constituents will see you as taking money away from them. The president is the only elected official whose constituents have no one else to share costs with. He is therefore the only elected official to whom projects which are not cost-effective are clearly political liabilities. If we are serious about weeding waste out of government, he is the best weeder we've got and we ought to be giving him more power.

However, much as we need to give the president more budgetary power, we must be careful not to give him *too much* power, or to allow him to channel it in the wrong direction. The president is not only the chief executive of the land, he is also the chief politician. Like all politicians he must roll logs frantically to get what he wants; and he probably has certain ideological commitments which, though they may endear him to us and help him get elected, can also lead him down the garden path at budget time, causing him to advocate projects and programs that are fiscally irresponsible but ideologically irresistible.

One need go no further back than the fall of 1979 and the famous incident in which President Carter's Transportation Department withheld discretionary funds from Chicago because Mayor Jane Byrne announced her support of Ted Kennedy's drive for the presidency to see how presidential control over the budget can be sadly abused at the present level, let alone the level we are suggesting that it be jumped to. Presidents have always done this sort of thing. Before Jimmy Carter there was Gerald Ford, whose Transportation Department, in an astonishingly similar ploy, took a $400-million mass-transit grant that probably should have gone to Denver and gave it to Detroit instead, at a point in the 1976 election campaign where Colorado remained solidly Republican but Michigan appeared to be wavering toward the Democrats. Before Gerald Ford there was Jack Kennedy, whose free hand with patronage for Massachusetts helped boost brother Ted into the Senate in the first place. Kennedy family sources deny that this sort of hanky-panky went on, but there seems little real doubt that it did. A reporter for *Life* magazine told of standing outside the White House with an administration official in 1962 and watching Kennedy aide Dick Donahue climb into a car and head off to Boston to work on Teddy's campaign. "There goes a man with twenty-six post offices in his back pocket," the official remarked candidly.

We must also, in our search for presidential power over the budget, guard against the Nixonian practice of manhandling the intent of Congress by the massive withholding of funds for programs which Congress has overwhelmingly approved but which the president, for one reason or another, happens not to like. Nixon did this by simply refusing to allow his executive agencies to spend the money that Congress had given to them for certain programs, a process known as impoundment. Congress has since enacted strict controls over impoundment, a wise and long-overdue move.

"Nixon was hoarding away all that money," points out Common Cause's Bruce Adams, "and Congress, I think properly, said, 'Look, pal—we pass it, you spend it.' So they set up the impoundment controls. And you can make the argument that that's too bad, because good old Carter could have impounded some money for some of these water projects, and we'd all be better off. But there's a bigger institutional question at stake here. I don't think it's an adequate answer to say, 'Well, let's go back to the days of impoundments now that we've got Jimmy Carter who's going to impound things we don't want, as opposed to Richard Nixon, who was stopping things we wanted.' It takes away a certain amount of the power that the president had, but nevertheless, it was a legitimate reform." Adams is right. No one wants to return to the politics of the Nixon era. Is a line-item veto too dangerous?

Possibly. Not, however, very likely. There are two very good reasons to be optimistic about the line-item veto's inability to be misused by a greedy or willful president. First, it would be a *budgetary* line-item veto, limited to specific items on appropriations bills, and thus could not be used to twist the intent of Congress on policy-making legislation or other forms of substantive law. Second, it would be a budgetary line-item *veto*. A veto is not an impoundment, and must not be mistaken for one. An impoundment is a constitutionally questionable tool used by presidents to defy the will of Congress. A veto is neither constitutionally questionable nor, strictly speaking, an act of defiance (though it may be mistaken for one). A veto is a presidential power specifically granted and explicitly spelled out by the Constitution to provide some means of reining back an unruly and headstrong Congress. There is nothing new or mysterious about a veto. Congress meets them on a regular basis, and it knows how to deal with them. An impoundment can come at any time and for any amount, and can leave congressmen with nothing to do beyond gnashing their teeth and exhausting their vocabularies. A veto can come only at the time of a bill's passage, and when one comes Congress immediately gets another crack at the item of disagreement. I may be overly optimistic, but I believe strongly that the chances for misuse of a budgetary line-item veto are very small, and that they are far outweighed by the advantages that would accrue from the veto's adoption.

If, however, you don't agree—if the Nixon spectre still haunts you, if the Imperial Presidency lurks under your covers at night, if you wish the power of the president curbed yet further rather than expanded, even ever so cautiously—then perhaps you might like my second suggestion better. Like the first, it proposes to use the pork ethic against itself by giving a national constituency greater power over the legislative process, with the idea that the broader self-interest of the national constituency will tend to override the narrow, parochial self-interests of the individual localities. Unlike the first, however, this second suggestion does not promote any single elected official or group of officials to a position of greater power. It doesn't work by altering the relation between the legislative and executive branches of government. In fact, it doesn't touch the legislative and executive branches at all, except indirectly. What it does, instead, is grant power to the national electorate in the most direct way possible: by giving it, through the processes of initiative and referendum, a direct vote and a direct voice in the making of some of the nation's laws.

"The theory behind this," says NTU's David Keating, "is that if you could let the people pass a statute or propose an initiative, they could take a vote on these pork-barrel projects—the country as a whole—and eliminate them pretty easily and quickly. Get a certain number of signatures, get it on the ballot, and have the people vote on it. Because what you really need is just a lot of people with common sense."

Again, we must be careful. There are certain dangers to the voter-initiative process, dangers which the framers of the Constitution were undoubtedly aware of when they left it out. It would be tremendously cumbersome, for one thing. Merely collecting and verifying enough voters' signatures to qualify an initiative for the national ballot would be a task to make strong men weep. After that would be the campaigning, and the policing of the campaigning to keep it within some semblance of honesty; then the vote and the tabulation of the vote. It would take months, perhaps years, for each initiative, even with modern communications equipment. It would also require an informed electorate, something that is impossible to guarantee. The congressional filtration system—hearings, markup sessions, floor debate—would be bypassed for a good old American rough-and-tumble political campaign, and we all know how *those* go. Political campaigns are, by their very nature, wide open to propaganda, and there is a real danger that the winner of an initiative campaign will turn out not to be the side with the strongest position but the side with the best advertising agency, as with California's New Melones Dam.

Finally, there is an extremely serious threat of voter burn-out, especially in those states which already have some form of statewide initiative process. As any voter in one of those states will tell you, there is something downright intimidating about walking into a voting booth and coming up against a ballot the size of a bedsheet, with several dozen candidates and a score of ballot measures, each of which you are supposed to be knowledgeable enough about to be able to cast an intelligent vote. Voter apathy is bad enough even in those areas where they don't put people through *that* wringer. Can the right to vote take the shock of a voter initiative and still survive?

Maybe not, but it seems worth the chance. Because Keating is right: A voter-initiative amendment would be the beginning of the end for the pork barrel. If the taxpayers who must foot the bills were asked if they really wanted to continue to shell out in order to build a canal for Du Pont, a harbor for Warren G. Magnuson, four destroyers that the navy doesn't want and can't use, and so forth, what do you think they'd answer? Is there any real doubt that they'd vote these things down? Is there any doubt that we would have entered an era where a public-works project would have to be able to strictly justify itself—would have to stick to Bruce Adams's criteria that are not being stuck to—or risk being turned down by an angry electorate that was tired of seeing its money wasted? The pork ethic can only operate in a country made up of numerous small, discrete constituencies. Tear the barriers down between those constituencies, lump them together in a single electorate, and pork is powerless. The barrel will stop rolling when there is no one left to roll it to.

And it may not be necessary to suffer the drawbacks of the voter-initiative process to obtain its advantages. There are ways of getting around the hazards, ways of wording the amendment so that it will fly straight to the green and not fall into the sandtraps on either side. To begin with, there should probably be an upper limit—fifteen seems about right—on the number of initiatives that could qualify for any given ballot. That ought to take care of the bedsheet-ballot syndrome. To avoid the inclusion on the ballot of measures concerning issues of intense parochial concern but yawning national indifference, there should be a requirement that initiative petitions bear the signatures of at least 2 percent of the registered voters in each of at least three-fourths of the states of the union. A public-funding clause written into the amendment could go a long way toward preventing a disastrous advertising-agency battle from taking the place of a healthy campaign.

Finally, there should almost certainly be language in the amendment limiting the initiative process strictly to laws affecting only the internal affairs of the United States. I make this last point with some reluctance. Like many others of my generation (I was born in 1942), I first came to political consciousness through the questionable offices of the war in Vietnam, and while that little monstrosity was underway I certainly would have welcomed the opportunity to stop it through the initiative process. Sober consideration, however, tells me that such an approach would have been wrong. Elections— national or local, ballot measure or elective office—are too often won or lost solely on emotions. The conduct of foreign affairs is no place for emotions. Negotiators among nations must be free to negotiate without fear that the folks back home will come running in and upset the apple cart before all the apples are sold. While an informed and angry electorate might get us out of a war we should not be in, it might just as easily get us into one. This must not be risked under any circumstances. The initiative procedure must not allow an electorate that is angry because the U.S. lost a gymnastics competition to order a bomb dropped on Moscow. The initiative procedure must mind its own business.

Will we get an initiative procedure that can mind anybody's business? David Keating thinks so. "It's coming," he told me, in that brave little converted ghetto townhouse in Washington. "Sometime. It may take fifty years, but it's coming. We already have twenty-three states that have voter-initiative powers, and more and more states are adding on to that. And someday you'll get thirty-odd states that have that power, and somebody will do just what we did with the balanced budget. Go through those states and get them to petition for a constitutional convention. And then

you might see Congress act." Is Keating right? I hope so.
The initiative process just might be the best weapon against
pork barreling that we could get. I'm not sure we can afford
to keep it in the holster much longer.

And Keating is probably right on another point, too—
that Congress will not act on this or any other reform
without the threat of a constitutional convention. It might,
but I'm not going to hold my breath to find out. Congress's
performance on reform does not encourage breath holding. It is not just the way in which the pork barrel rolled
over Jimmy Carter in 1979 that makes me say that. It is the
whole dismal record of the last two hundred years.

- In 1978, the year of Carter's "victory" over the pork barrel, Congress defeated a bill sponsored by Senator William Proxmire to cut off funding and require reauthorization of any project which had cost overruns of more than
  50 percent. As Grover Norquist of NTU pointed out, this
  defeat means that competitive bidding is meaningless on
  government work because you can submit a bid at any
  ridiculously low level you wish, secure in the knowledge
  that once you get the contract nobody's going to hold you
  to the bid anyway—Congress will cheerfully fork over anything extra you ask for. Try that on the private sector and
  see how far you get.
- In 1977, a House committee killed, and Senator Howard
  Baker filibustered to death, a set of campaign-finance reforms that would have gone a long way toward breaking
  the congressman–special interest connection which
  makes up the left-hand leg of the Iron Triangle.
- In 1976, Congress actually passed a major piece of reform
  legislation, the Congressional Budget Act of 1976, and
  then proceeded to ignore most of it and continue with
  business as usual. To most congressmen, the Budget Act
  seems to have been primarily an opportunity to gain
  points with their constituents. "The beauty of the budget
  process," one has remarked, is that "you can vote for all

the appropriations and then vote against the deficit." The two votes may be totally irreconcilable if placed side by side, but no one in Congress ever does that. They all want to have their cake and eat it too.

● In 1975 . . . but why bother?

The point is that in almost any year you can find a congressional reform that failed. The problem, simply put, is one of handles. Congress has them all and doesn't want to give any of them up. Power flow in American government has always been inward—in to Washington, in to Congress, in to the committees. Any move that attempts to reverse that flow, or even to slow it down, is going to be met with downright hostility.

But it may not be so hard after all. Because as powerful as the pork-barrel system is, it is only as powerful as Congress allows it to be. And as powerful as Congress is, it is only as powerful as we allow it to be. That is the ace up our sleeve, the card that may yet save us. Pork makes waste, Congress makes pork—but we make Congress. And ultimately, if we care enough, that power to make Congress will build us a Congress that will back off from the pork barrel and take a long look around, a Congress that will discover how to live low on the hog, a Congress that can build us a new nation, one that is compassionate, just, wealthy, strong—and lean.

Selected Bibliography

BOOKS

(This list by no means exhausts the field of books that a student of pork barreling will find useful, but it gives a good general idea of the ground from which the ideas presented in this book grew.)

Ashworth, William. *Hells Canyon: The Deepest Gorge on Earth.* New York: Hawthorn Books, Inc., 1977.

Bailey, Stephen K., and Samuel, Howard D. *Congress at Work.* New York: Henry Holt and Co., 1952.

Clement, Thomas M., Jr.; Lopez, Glen; and Mountain, Pamela T. *Engineering a Victory for Our Environment: A Citizen's Guide to the U.S. Army Corps of Engineers.* San Francisco: Sierra Club Books, 1973.

Coffin, Tristram. *The Passion of the Hawks: Militarism in Modern America.* New York: The Macmillan Co., 1964.

Fenno, Richard F., Jr. *The Power of the Purse: Appropriations Politics in Congress.* Boston: Little, Brown and Co., 1966.

Ferejohn, John A. *Pork Barrel Politics: Rivers and Harbors Legislation, 1947–1968.* Stanford, California: Stanford University Press, 1974.

Fochs, Arnold. *Advertising That Won Elections.* Duluth, Minnesota: A. J. Publishing Co., 1974.

Froman, Lewis A., Jr. *The Congressional Process.* Boston: Little, Brown and Co., 1967.

Gardner, John W. *In Common Cause.* New York: W. W. Norton, Inc., 1972.

Green, Mark J., ed. *The Monopoly Makers.* New York: Grossman Publishers, 1973.

Green, Mark J.; Fallowes, James M.; and Zwick, David R. *Who Runs Congress?* New York: Bantam Books, Inc., 1972.

Heuvelmans, Martin. *The River Killers.* Harrisburg, Pennsylvania: Stackpole Books, 1974.

Horn, Stephen. *Unused Power: The Work of the Senate Committee on Appropriations.* Washington, D.C.: The Brookings Institution, 1970.

Kelly, Alfred H., and Harbison, Winfred A. *The American Constitution: Its Origins and Development.* 4th ed. New York: W. W. Norton & Co., Inc., 1970.

Lambro, Donald. *The Federal Rathole.* New Rochelle, New York: Arlington House Publishers, 1975.

MacNeill, Neil. *Forge of Democracy: The House of Representatives.* New York: David McKay Company, Inc., 1963.

Marine, Gene. *America the Raped.* New York: Avon Books, Inc., 1969.

Milbraith, Lester W. *The Washington Lobbyists.* Chicago: Rand McNally, Inc., 1963.

Ognibene, Peter J. *Scoop: The Life and Politics of Henry M. Jackson.* New York: Stein and Day, Publishers, 1975.

Pearson, Drew, and Anderson, Jack. *The Case Against Congress.* New York: Simon & Schuster, 1968.

Plano, Jack C., and Greenburg, Milton. *The American Political Dictionary.* New York: Holt, Rinehart and Winston, Inc., 1967.

Reservoirs, Problems and Conflicts. Corvallis, Oregon: Water Resources Research Institute, Oregon State University, 1969.

Smith, Frank E. *The Politics of Conservation.* New York: Pantheon Books, 1966.

Sperber, Hans, and Trittschuh, Travis. *American Political Terms: An Historical Dictionary.* Detroit: Wayne State University Press, 1962.

Todd, David Keith, ed. *The Water Encyclopedia.* Port Washington, New York: Water Information Center, 1970.

Washington: City and Capital. Washington, D. C.: Federal Writers' Project, Works Progress Administration, 1937.

Weaver, Warren. *Both Your Houses: The Truth about Congress.* New York: Praeger Publishing Co., 1972.

Wertheimer, Fred, et al. *How Money Talks in Congress.* Washington, D.C.: Common Cause, 1979.

Wildavsky, Aaron. *The Politics of the Budgetary Process.* 3d ed. Boston: Little, Brown and Co., 1979.

Wright, Jim. *You and Your Congressman.* Revised ed. New York: Coward,
    McCann & Geoghegan, Inc., 1972.

ANNUAL AND BIENNIAL PUBLICATIONS

(Almanacs, yearbooks, annual reports of government agencies, statistical compilations, and the like. It is from these that the factual data
concerning the scope and impact of pork barreling can most easily be
derived. Those that I list are the ones I found particularly useful; no
attempt has been made to be exhaustive.)

Annual Report of the Chief of Engineers for Civil Works Activities. Washington,
    D.C.: Department of the Army, Corps of Engineers. (annual)
Barone, Michael; Ujifusa, Grant; and Matthews, Douglas. *The Almanac of
    American Politics.* New York: E. P. Dutton. (biennial)
The Budget of the United States Government. Washington, D.C.: U.S. Govern-
    ment Printing Office. (annual)
Congressional District Data Book. Washington, D.C.: U.S. Department of
    Commerce, Bureau of the Census. (annual)
Congressional Quarterly Almanac. Washington, D.C.: Congressional Quar-
    terly, Inc. (biennial)
Federal Aid to States. Washington, D.C.: Department of the Treasury.
    (annual)
Federal Reclamation Projects: Water and Land Resource Accomplishments. Wash-
    ington, D.C.: U.S. Department of the Interior, Bureau of Reclama-
    tion. (annual)
Statistical Abstract of the United States. Washington, D.C.: U.S. Department
    of Commerce, Bureau of the Census. (annual)
United States Government Manual. Washington, D.C.: Office of the Federal
    Register, National Archives and Records Service, General Services
    Administration. (annual)
Waterborne Commerce of the United States. Washington, D.C.: Department of
    the Army, Corps of Engineers. (annual)

PERIODICALS

(Had I included an entry for every newspaper or magazine article I used,
I would have created a bibliography nearly as long as the book itself.
There are also many articles in scholarly journals and in national mass-
circulation monthlies that I found useful, not to mention the great variety of public-interest lobby-group publications, which run the gamut
from the carefully crafted and superbly produced *Audubon* magazine to
the offset-on-typewriter-paper *Tennes-Sierran.*

Below is a selection, admittedly an arbitrary one, of fifty sources in this category. I have tried to achieve a balance among articles on different types of pork barreling, articles on different aspects of pork barreling and articles from different types of periodicals. The resulting list, I think, shows a good cross-section of the periodical sources used in researching this book.

Page, issue, and volume numbers were not always available, sometimes because my notes were incomplete and sometimes because the source itself failed to use these numbers. In the interest of consistency, I have eliminated them throughout the list, relying on the date of publication to guide the reader to the right article. Where local newspapers are cited, the news service or feature syndicate from which the newspaper received the item is given in parentheses. Newspaper items without this parenthetical source citation originated with the cited newspaper itself.)

Adams, Gordon. "Hooked on Defense Spending." (*Christian Science Monitor* News Service.) *The Daily Tidings*, Ashland, Oregon, February 5, 1979.

"Annual Voting Study Unmasks Government Spending." *Dollars and Sense*, July 1979.

Ballard, John E. "Federal Reservoirs and Community Effects." *American Rivers*, December 1977.

"Benefits Flow Downstream." *American Rivers*, December 1977.

"Billion Dollar Corps Projects Bill Dammed." *Washington Resource Report*, November 1978.

"Breaking the Special Interest Stranglehold on Congress." *Sierra Club National News Report*, August 31, 1979.

Cahn, Robert. "The Triumph of Wrong." *Audubon*, November 1979.

Cassidy, John. "A Man and a River." *Not Man Apart*, June 1979.

Clark, Timothy B. "Beekeepers Abuzz over Budget." *National Journal*, March 3, 1979.

"Court Disclosures Revive Push to Kill Waterway." *Sierra Club National News Report*, May 11, 1979.

"Election Year Pork Barrel Politics Give Water Project Benefits to a Few." *Washington Resource Report*, September 1978.

"The Federal Budget and the Environment." *Sierra Club National News Report*, April 26, 1979.

"Fort Dix May March Off into Oblivion." (UPI.) *The Daily Tidings*, Ashland, Oregon, March 30, 1979.

Free, James. "Flood Control Works in Reverse, Groups Say." *The Birmingham News*, Birmingham, Alabama, April 25, 1979.

Furgurson, Ernest B. "Staving Off the Ferocious Snail Darter." (Los

Angeles *Times* News Syndicate.) The Seattle *Times*, September 18, 1979.

Gardner, Don. "The Trinity River: Water and Politics." *The Texas Observer*, May 20, 1979.

Garrison, Charles B. "A Case Study of the Local Economic Impact of Reservoir Recreation." *Journal of Leisure Research*, Winter 1974.

"Great Lakes Winter Navigation: Gilding U.S. Steel's Lily." *Sierra Club National News Report*, June 22, 1979.

Hannon, Bruce, and Bezdek, Roger. "Job Impact of Alternatives to Corps of Engineers Projects." *Engineering Issues*, October 1973.

Holzman, David. "SPS—The Road to Disaster in Solar Power." *Oregon Conifer*, May 1979.

"House Moves into Solar Orbit." *Sierra Club National News Report*, December 7, 1979.

"House Sustains Veto of Carter Public Works Bill." *Facts on File*, October 13, 1978.

Jarvis, Howard. "Howard Jarvis Says 'It's an Outrage!' " (advertisement). *The Washington Post*, October 5, 1978.

"Jobs and the Environment." *Friends' Committee on National Legislation Washington Newsletter*, May 1979.

Klaidman, Stephen. "Conflict Snarls Midwest Waterway Expansion." *The Washington Post*, July 7, 1975.

————. "Engineer Corps: Benefits Contested." *The Washington Post*, July 6, 1975.

Laycock, George. "A Dam is Not Difficult to Build Unless It Is in the Wrong Place." *Audubon*, November 1976.

McBride, Bob, and DuBois, Mark. "Save This River." *Headwaters*, June 1979.

McGrory, Mary. "Senator Long Stands by Carter, but He's Cause of Energy Problems." (Washington *Star* Syndicate.) *The Daily Tidings*, Ashland, Oregon, June 15, 1979.

"Military Cuts Hurt a Bit, but We Need Them." *The Daily Tidings*, Ashland, Oregon, March 31, 1979.

"Military Streamlining Plan Draws Outrage, Opposition." (UPI.) *The Daily Tidings*, Ashland, Oregon, March 30, 1979.

"Mount Sexton Station Goes Back in Budget." *The Daily Tidings*, Ashland, Oregon, June 4, 1979.

"Music Career for Senator Byrd?" (UPI.) *The Daily Tidings*, Ashland, Oregon, August 21, 1979.

"News Flash: Duncan Dumps Darter." *The Tennes-Sierran*, July–August 1979.

"No Sales Tax Boost for Carlyle." *American Rivers*, December 1977.

"Preparing for the 700-year Flood." *Sierra Club National News Report*, May 11, 1979.

"President Seizes Initiative in Water Policy." *Washington Resource Report*, November 1978.

"Reappraise Stonewall." Charleston *Daily Mail*, Charleston, West Virginia, November 15, 1978.

Reed, Leonard. "The Budget Game and How to Win It." *Washington Monthly*, January 1979.

"Salty Colorado Sets Boondoggle Solution Afloat." *Sierra Club National News Report*, August 17, 1979.

Sinclair, Ward. "The Hill Has Moved to Shred Carter's New Water Policy." *The Washington Post*, August 29, 1978.

———. "Hill Pork Barrel Won't Hold Water." *The Washington Post*, October 23, 1978.

———. "Stennis Advice Kills Hearing on Waterway." *The Washington Post*, May 12, 1979.

Smith, Courtland L.; Hogg, Thomas C.; and Reagan, Michael J. "Economic Development: Panacea or Perplexity for Rural Areas?" *Rural Sociology*, June 1971.

"Tellico Dam: Four Decades of Pork Politics." *Sierra Club National News Report*, August 17, 1979.

"A Time to Choose: Synthetic Fuels and the American Future." *Oregon Conifer*, August 1979.

"Trans-Alaska Pipeline Opens." *Facts on File*, June 25, 1977.

"Umpqua Lighthouse is Dedicated." (UPI.) *The Daily Tidings*, Ashland, Oregon, August 21, 1979.

"Waterway User Fee Sold Down River." *Washington Resource Report*, November 1978.

Wheeler, Keith; Suydam, Henry; Ritter, Norman; Wise, Bill; and Sochurek, Howard. "Now—See the Innards of a Fat Pig." *Life*, August 16, 1963.

BOOKLETS, BROCHURES, PAMPHLETS, AND PAPERS

(This category contains a selection of materials which I found useful and which fail to fit into any of the other categories of this bibliography. As with Annual and Biennial Publications, this is but a partial list of information sources in this category that I used in writing this book.)

The Army Corps of Engineers and Environmental Conservation: Nine Questions. Washington, D.C.: Department of the Army, Office of the Chief of Engineers, 1971.

Blackwelder, Brent. *Benefit Claims of the Water Development Agencies: The Need for Continuing Reform.* Washington, D.C.: Environmental Policy Institute, 1976.

——. *Citizen's Guide to the New Carter Water Policy.* Washington, D.C.: Environmental Policy Center, 1978.

Blackwelder, Brent, and Carlson, Peter. *An Analysis of the Stonewall Jackson Lake Project of the U.S. Army Corps of Engineers.* Washington, D.C.: Environmental Policy Center, 1979.

Campbell, Thomas C. *Testimony Relative to the Stonewall Jackson Lake Project.* Senate Judiciary Committee Hearings, Charleston, West Virginia, February 22, 1979.

Cicchetti, Charles J., et al. *Benefits or Costs? An Assessment of the Water Resources Council's Proposed Principles and Standards.* Baltimore, Maryland: Johns Hopkins University Press, 1972.

A Citizens Action Guide to the Federal Flood Insurance Program. Washington, D.C.: American Rivers Conservation Council, 1974.

"Common Cause President Cites Special Interest Role in Inflation." Washington, D.C.: Common Cause news release, June 18, 1979.

Disasters in Water Development. Washington, D.C.: American Rivers Conservation Council, 1977.

Holubetz, Terry, and Simons, Richard. *Distribution of Recreationists on Impounded and Unimpounded Sectors of the Lower Columbia and Snake Rivers.* Idaho Department of Fish and Game, 1973.

"How Congress Voted on Energy and the Environment: 1978 Voting Chart." Washington, D.C.: League of Conservation Voters, 1979.

League of Conservation Voters 1978 Election Report. Washington, D.C.: League of Conservation Voters, 1979.

Moncrief, Nancye, and Mong, Bob. "A Big Dam Mess." Cincinnati, Ohio: Cincinnati *Post* Reprint, 1974.

95 Theses. Washington, D.C.: American Rivers Conservation Council and Environmental Policy Center, 1974.

Osann, Ed, and Curran, Diane. *Who Pays for Pork?* Washington, D.C.: National Wildlife Federation, 1978.

Wilson, E. Raymond; Neely, Frances E.; and Longshore, Constance. *The Big Hand in Your Pocket: Your Taxes, Your Livelihood, and the Growing Power of the Military.* Washington, D.C.: Friends' Committee on National Legislation, 1960.

A NOTE ON UNCITED SOURCES

Two types of source that I found particularly useful in researching and shaping the text do not appear in this bibliography. One is the many personal interviews I had with people deeply involved in the pork-barrel system. These, I believe, have been adequately taken care of in the text itself and in the Acknowledgments. The second category is that of congressional documents—hearings records, committee reports, journals— and here I plead guilty to simply throwing up my hands in despair. Far too much material pours out of the congressional paper mill each year for any partial list to be meaningful, or any meaningful list to be attainable. Nevertheless, for those who wish to pursue this particular aspect of pork research, certain guidelines may be given. The best direct sources for researching Congress and the pork barrel are, in order of importance, hearings records (especially those of the House and Senate Appropriations Committees, Public Works Committees, and Defense Committees), the pages of the *Congressional Record* around appropriations time, and the committee reports on appropriations bills, omnibus authorization bills, military procurement bills, and budget resolutions. These are available from any of the many libraries nationwide which are designated government depositories. Ask your librarian.

Index

Aberbach, Joel, 27, 91, 113, 114, 162
"access," as issue, 136, 171
Adams, Bruce, 11, 159, 170, 173, 181
Adams, Gordon, 152
Advertising That Won Elections (Fochs), 30
aerospace industry, 19
agencies, federal, 10–11, 12, 25
    as "agencies of Congress," 43
    anti-pork efforts of, 140–141
    appropriations process and, 57, 58
    congressional committees and, 22–24, 58, 88–89
    crossover employment and, 134–137, 138–139
    direct pressure by, 130–131
    essential weakness of, 139, 141–142
    as information source, 130, 132–133, 137–138
    in Iron Triangle, 104–105
    lobby pressures vs., 140
    logrolling and, 79, 80–81
    manipulative techniques used by, 128–134
    as mission-oriented, 124–128
    priorities in, 1, 15–17
agricultural interests, 9
Agriculture Department, U.S., 23, 127
Alaska Pipeline, 35–36, 37–38
Allott, Gordon, 30
American Political Dictionary (Plano and Greenburg), 27
AMTRAK, 17, 78–79
Anderson, Jack, 5
Andrus, Cecil, 165
Animal Farm (Orwell), 29
Applegate Dam, 132–133

197